MultiMedia Guide to Accompany

EDUCATIONAL PSYCHOLOGY
Developing Learners

Fourth Edition

Jeanne Ellis Ormrod

University of Northern Colorado (Emerita)

University of New Hampshire

Upper Saddle River, New Jersey
Columbus, Ohio

Instructors of classes using Ormrod, *Educational Psychology: Developing Learners, Fourth Edition,* may reproduce material from the multimedia guide for classroom use.

10 9 8 7 6 5 4 3 2 1

ISBN: 0-13-088707-2

PREFACE

Accompanying the fourth edition of *Educational Psychology: Developing Learners* are several multimedia supplements:

- *Simulations in Educational Psychology:* This CD, which is packaged with the book, offers five simulated activities through which students can explore concepts and principles related to learning, child development, and assessment.

- Student Artifact Library: This Internet-based virtual "library" contains more than 100 examples of student schoolwork (writing samples, math problems, artwork, etc.) and teacher products (assignments, tests, reports to parents, etc.). The artifacts illustrate numerous principles related to learning processes, developmental trends, motivation, and classroom strategies.

- Companion Website: This Website augments each chapter of the book with a glossary, self-test questions, and links to Internet sites relevant to chapter content. It also provides a Syllabus Manager™ and Message Board through which instructors and students can communicate regularly.

- Nine videotapes: These videotapes show students and teachers in action in elementary, middle school, and secondary classrooms.

- *Educator Learning Center:* The result of a collaboration between Merrill Education and the Association of Supervision and Curriculum Development (ASCD), this Website provides Internet access to an ever-growing collection of *Educational Leadership* articles, case studies, instructional strategies and lesson plans, simulations, tutorials, and videos.

- *PowerPoint Slides and Supplementary Lectures and Activities:* This CD provides electronic versions of the activities, lectures, handouts, and transparency masters that appear in this guide and in the *Instructor's Manual* that also accompanies the book.

In this guide I offer my suggestions for how you might effectively use these media to supplement class materials and enhance classroom instruction.

J.E.O.

TABLE OF CONTENTS

USING *POWERPOINT SLIDES AND SUPPLEMENTARY LECTURES AND ACTIVITIES*

An instructor's compact disk entitled *PowerPoint Slides and Supplementary Lectures and Activities* accompanies *Educational Psychology: Developing Learners*. The CD includes the following:

- **Test Bank:**
  - Multiple-choice and essay questions for the sixteen textbook chapters (Microsoft Word documents)
  - Integrative multiple-choice and essay questions that draw on content from two or more of the textbook chapters (Microsoft Word document)
  - Multiple-choice questions for Appendix A (Microsoft Word document)
  - Multiple-choice and essay questions for Supplementary Readings #1–#7 in the *Study Guide and Reader* (Microsoft Word document)
  - Multiple-choice and essay questions for "Learning in the Content Areas," located both in the *Study Guide and Reader* (Supplementary Reading #8) and on the Companion Website (Microsoft Word document)

- **Materials from the *Instructor's Manual:***
  - Supplementary lectures (Microsoft Word documents)
  - Suggested activities (Microsoft Word documents)
  - Handouts (Microsoft PowerPoint documents)
  - Transparency masters (Microsoft PowerPoint documents)

- **Transparencies:** Electronic copies of the acetate transparencies (Microsoft PowerPoint documents)

- **Materials from this *MultiMedia Guide:***
  - Handouts (Microsoft PowerPoint documents)
  - Transparency masters (Microsoft PowerPoint documents)

- **Link to the Student Artifact Library**

You will find folders for each of these when you insert the CD into your computer.

USING THE COMPANION WEBSITE

You can find the Companion Website for *Educational Psychology: Developing Learners* at www.prenhall.com/ormrod. The Website includes the following features:

- **Navigation bar:** Menu buttons are located at the left side of the screen to provide easy access to the various parts of the Website.

- **Syllabus Manager™:** The Syllabus Manager™ allows you to create and put your syllabus directly on the Website. It highlights class meeting dates in white and assignment due dates in blue. Students can access your syllabus if they know the address for the Companion Website and the password you have assigned to your syllabus.
  You can revise your syllabus as often as you need to. For instance, you can easily add or modify an assignment by clicking on the desired due date and filling in the details. In addition, links to other activities can be created easily. If the activity is online, a URL can be entered in the space provided, and it will be automatically linked in the final syllabus. Students will see your revisions immediately the next time they log on to the Website. Students can link to assignments on the Companion Website or the Web from the syllabus. Your completed syllabus is hosted on Prentice Hall servers, allowing convenient updates from any computer on the Internet.

- **Chapter features:** For each chapter, the Website lists central questions that the chapter will address, a chapter glossary, and Internet Websites related to chapter content. Furthermore, students can take a quick self-test (in the form of sample multiple-choice and essay questions), get hints about where to find answers to each question, and receive feedback about their performance.

- **Supplementary readings:** The eight supplementary readings in the *Study Guide and Reader* are presented on the Companion Website as well.

- **Link to the Student Artifact Library:** This virtual "library" is an electronic collection of student schoolwork (e.g., writing samples, math assignments, artwork) and teacher artifacts (e.g., assignments, tests). (See the succeeding section, "Using the Student Artifact Library.")

- **Message board:** Easily accessed from any chapter, the message board provides a place where students can communicate with one another and exchange ideas related to course content. For example, you might pose a controversial question and ask students to respond. Some discussion topics listed in the *Instructor's Manual* have been posted on this site.

- **Feedback button:** Here you and your students can give the people at Merrill Education and Prentice Hall ongoing feedback about the usefulness of the Website.

A transparency master listing these features (Transparency MG.1) can be found among the "Handout Masters" both at the end of this manual and on the instructor's CD *PowerPoint Slides and Supplementary Lectures and Activities* .

USING THE STUDENT ARTIFACT LIBRARY

The Student Artifact Library is an electronic "library" containing more than 100 examples of student schoolwork (e.g., writing samples, math assignments, artwork) and teacher artifacts (e.g., assignments, tests, feedback to parents). It is a Web-based database that can be accessed either from the textbook's Companion Website (www.prenhall.com/ormrod) or from the instructor CD *PowerPoint Slides and Supplementary Lectures and Activities.*

The artifacts in the library are categorized by both grade level and content domain. When you get to the first screen on the Website, you will be asked to make a "Grade Selection" from the following choices:
- Preschool
- Grades K–2
- Grades 3–5
- Grades 6–8
- Grades 9–12
- Teacher Artifacts

Once you have made your selection, you will then be asked to make a "Content Selection," as follows:
   a. If you have previously selected Preschool, Grades K-2, Grades 3-5, Grades 6-8, or Grades 9-12, you will then be asked to select one of the following:
      - Math
      - Language Arts/Reading
      - Science
      - Social Studies
      - Art & Music
      - Personal and Social Development & Thinking Skills
   a. If you have previously selected Teacher Artifacts, you will then be asked to select one of the following:
      - Preschool
      - Grades K-2
      - Grades 3-5
      - Grades 6-8
      - Grades 9-12

After you have made a content selection, you will see a screen in which relevant artifacts are listed by ID number. Click on the appropriate number to view a particular artifact. You can print out an artifact by clicking on the "Print" button.

You can use the artifacts to illustrate concepts and principles from various chapters and to create "Interpreting Artifacts and Interactions" exercises similar to those found in the textbook. The *Instructor's Manual* identifies one or more artifacts that may be especially relevant to each chapter in the textbook. In some cases, you might ask your students to analyze artifacts as out-of-class assignments. In other cases, you might use them to stimulate small-group or whole-class discussions.

Contents of the Student Artifact Library

The following table briefly describes some of the artifacts included in the library at the time this manual goes to press in the spring of 2002. (The library will continue to grow in the months and years that follow, so the table will be incomplete by the time you use this manual.) The right-hand column in the table indicates which artifacts are described further in the *Instructor's Manual.*

I have organized the topics by grade level and then by content domain (with "Teacher Artifact" included in the "Content Domain" column). Note that some artifacts have been classified as belonging to more than one content area (e.g., they might be both "Science" and "Teacher Artifact") and so appear more than once in the table.

Grade Level	Content Domain	ID #	Brief Description	Suggestions in *Instr.'s Manual?*
Preschl	Math	01	Tracing numerals 1 and 2	
Preschl	Math	02	Circles worksheet; early practice in counting	
Preschl	Math	04	Matching objects to numerals	
Preschl	Math	03	Tracing numerals 1–5	
Preschl	Math	06	Place values worksheet	
Preschl	Lang. Arts	01	Pseudowriting (age 4)	
Preschl	Lang. Arts	02	Pseudowriting (age 5)	
Preschl	Lang. Arts	03	Early scribbles (precursor to handwriting)	
Preschl	Lang. Arts	04	Tracing numerals; early handwriting	
Preschl	Lang. Arts	09	Handwriting of name	
Preschl	Art & Music	01	Two-year-old's scribbles	
Preschl	Art & Music	02	Picture of traditional family and house	
Preschl	Art & Music	03	Tracing shapes	
Preschl	Pers./Soc./Think	01	Picture of traditional family and house	
Preschl	Teacher Artifact	01	Note home about tying shoes	
K-2	Math	01	Student writes own word problem	
K-2	Lang. Arts	01-02	Story, "How the parakeet got its name" (2 pp.)	
K-2	Lang. Arts	03	Story about best friend Miranda	yes (Ch. 3)
K-2	Lang. Arts	04	Story, "I am a maple seed"	
K-2	Lang. Arts	05	Handwriting, "I like to riyt."	
K-2	Lang. Arts	06	Essay about origins of U.S. (2nd grader)	yes (Ch. 2)
K-2	Lang. Arts	07	Description of new puppy, "Sky Way"	
K-2	Lang. Arts	08	Book report, shows writing disability	yes (Ch. 5)
K-2	Lang. Arts	09	Rough draft, "The Bear and the Horse"	
K-2	Lang. Arts	10	Making paragraphs, "The Bear and the Horse"	
K-2	Lang. Arts	11	Invented spelling, "I drew this pumpkin"	
K-2	Lang. Arts	12	Invented spelling, "Going to museum"	
K-2	Lang. Arts	13	Invented spelling, "This is my sister"	
K-2	Lang. Arts	14	Invented spelling, "Flying baseball"	
K-2	Lang. Arts	15	Handwriting, "One day Lonely was..."	
K-2	Lang. Arts	16	Letter to Abraham Lincoln	
K-2	Science	01	Apple tree	
K-2	Science	02	Underwater scene with scuba diver	
K-2	Science	03	Story, "I am a maple seed"	
K-2	Social Studies	02	Essay about origins of U.S. (2nd grader)	yes (Ch. 2)
K-2	Social Studies	03	Map of Loveland, CO (1st grader)	yes (Ch. 2)
K-2	Social Studies	04	Letter to Abraham Lincoln	
K-2	Art & Music	01	Fish with geometric shapes	

K-2	Art & Music	02	Underwater scene with scuba diver	
K-2	Art & Music	03	Whale in water	
K-2	Art & Music	04	Finger-painting of cat	
K-2	Art & Music	05	Drawings of different emotions (age 5)	
K-2	Art & Music	06	Picture of guitar	
K-2	Art & Music	07	Picture of girl with purse	
K-2	Art & Music	09	Picture of boy standing on hands	
K-2	Art & Music	10	Krista's drawing of herself and teacher	
K-2	Art & Music	11	Two boys' fantasy story on paper	
K-2	Art & Music	12	Map of Loveland, CO (1st grader)	yes (Ch. 2)
K-2	Art & Music	13	Picture and writing about two friends	
K-2	Art & Music	14	Drawing of pumpkin and bat	
K-2	Art & Music	15	Picture of skeleton	
K-2	Art & Music	16	Drawing of sister	
K-2	Art & Music	17	Drawing of flying baseball	
K-2	Pers./Soc./Think	02	Krista's drawing of herself and teacher	
K-2	Pers./Soc./Think	03	Painting of child sledding	
K-2	Pers./Soc./Think	04	Two boys' fantasy story on paper	
K-2	Pers./Soc./Think	05	Picture and writing about two friends	
K-2	Pers./Soc./Think	06	Letter to Abraham Lincoln	
K-2	Pers./Soc./Think	07	Finger-painting of cat	
K-2	Pers./Soc./Think	08	Drawings of different emotions (age 5)	
K-2	Pers./Soc./Think	09	Picture of girl with purse	
K-2	Pers./Soc./Think	11	Picture of boy standing on hands	
K-2	Pers./Soc./Think	12	Story about best friend Miranda	yes (Ch. 3)
K-2	Teacher Artifact	01	Note to parents about homework	yes (Ch. 13)
3-5	Math	01	Student writes own word problems	
3-5	Math	02	Diagram of number 34 as blocks	yes (Ch. 7)
3-5	Math	03	Addition error	
3-5	Math	04	Student writes own word problem	
3-5	Math	05	Student explains solution of 354 − 298	yes (Ch. 8)
3-5	Math	06	Student explains solution of 486 + 795	
3-5	Math	07	Explanation of multiplication; student has ADHD	yes (Ch. 5)
3-5	Lang. Arts	01	Song of myself ("I am Noah...")	
3-5	Lang. Arts	02	Spelling word families	
3-5	Lang. Arts	03	"How to play Crash Bandicot 2"	yes (Ch. 6)
3-5	Lang. Arts	04	Pledge of Allegiance misspelled	yes (Ch. 7)
3-5	Lang. Arts	05	Story, "The All Gone Meteor"	
3-5	Lang. Arts	06-08	Story of parents' divorce, "Two Moves..." (3 pp.)	
3-5	Lang. Arts	09	Cursive writing, "Speed Tests!"	yes (Ch. 11)
3-5	Lang. Arts	10-17	Historical fiction, "Moving to Ohio" (8 pp.)	
3-5	Lang. Arts	18	Reaction to "Roots"	yes (Ch. 11)
3-5	Lang. Arts	19	Letter to Thomas Jefferson	
3-5	Lang. Arts	20	Research paper, "Samuel de Champlain"	
3-5	Lang. Arts	21-22	Descriptive prose, "The wind whistled..."(2 pp.)	
3-5	Lang. Arts	24	Song of myself ("I am Shea...")	
3-5	Lang. Arts	25-26	Thank you letter plus working notes (2 pp.)	
3-5	Lang. Arts	27-28	Story, "My Tooth" (2 pp.)	
3-5	Lang. Arts	29-31	Descriptive prose, "Describing Snow" (3 pp.)	
3-5	Lang. Arts	32	Sailboat with alliterative sentence	yes (Ch. 2)
3-5	Lang. Arts	33	Handwriting, "All of a sudden..."	
3-5	Lang. Arts	34	Diary entry about physical abuse	
3-5	Lang. Arts	35	Essay about origins of U.S. (3rd grader)	yes (Ch. 2)

3-5	Lang. Arts	36	Writing about senses, "Dear Classmates"	
3-5	Lang. Arts	37	Writing spelling words in sentences	
3-5	Lang. Arts	38	Story about getting stitches	
3-5	Lang. Arts	39	Spelling test; student has mild learning disability	yes (Ch. 5)
3-5	Lang. Arts	40	Story, "The Crazy Turtle"	
3-5	Lang. Arts	41	Writing about friend, "Adventure Island"	
3-5	Lang. Arts	43	Handwriting, "When we left Greeley..."	
3-5	Lang. Arts	44	Handwriting, "Henry delivers..."	
3-5	Lang. Arts	45	Handwriting, "Have a good Mothers..."	
3-5	Science	01	Drawing of a seed growing	
3-5	Science	02	Chrysalis and butterfly	
3-5	Science	03	"A butterfly is..." with drawing	
3-5	Science	05-06	Thank you letter plus working notes (2 pp.)	
3-5	Science	07	Lab report, "Pig Lungs Dissection"	
3-5	Science	08	Eating from different food groups	yes (Ch. 10)
3-5	Science	09	Picture of children on playground	
3-5	Social Studies	01	Pledge of Allegiance misspelled	yes (Ch. 7)
3-5	Social Studies	02	Celebrating Christmas and Hanukkah	
3-5	Social Studies	03	Description, "Beds in 1621"	yes (Chs. 9, 16)
3-5	Social Studies	04-11	Historical fiction, "Moving to Ohio" (8 pp.)	
3-5	Social Studies	12	Reaction to "Roots"	yes (Ch. 11)
3-5	Social Studies	13	Letter to Thomas Jefferson	
3-5	Social Studies	14	Essay, "Why We Study History"	
3-5	Social Studies	15	Research paper, "Samuel de Champlain"	
3-5	Social Studies	16	Poster, "Purposes of State Governments"	
3-5	Social Studies	17	Letter to city council	
3-5	Social Studies	18	Essay about origins of U.S. (3rd grader)	yes (Ch. 2)
3-5	Social Studies	19	Map of Loveland, CO (3rd grader)	yes (Ch. 2)
3-5	Art & Music	01	Poppy field in watercolor	
3-5	Art & Music	02	Girl's face, "Portrait of a Friend"	
3-5	Art & Music	03	Multiple circles with designs	
3-5	Art & Music	04	Sailboat with alliterative sentence	yes (Ch. 2)
3-5	Art & Music	06	Ceramic family	
3-5	Art & Music	07	Picture of child in street with cars	
3-5	Art & Music	08	Cartoon showing argument and resolution	
3-5	Art & Music	09	Picture of boys in lunch line	
3-5	Art & Music	10	Assessment for general music	yes (Chs. 13, 16)
3-5	Art & Music	11	Rubric for watercolor collage	yes (Ch. 16)
3-5	Art & Music	12	Map of Loveland, CO (3rd grader)	yes (Ch. 2)
3-5	Pers./Soc./Think	01	Song of myself ("I am Noah...")	yes (Chs. xx, xx)
3-5	Pers./Soc./Think	02	Celebrating Christmas and Hanukkah	
3-5	Pers./Soc./Think	03	"Last nit I krid my self to slep."	
3-5	Pers./Soc./Think	04	Story, "The All Gone Meteor"	
3-5	Pers./Soc./Think	05-07	Story of parents' divorce, "Two Moves..." (3 pp.)	
3-5	Pers./Soc./Think	08	Cursive writing, "Speed Tests!"	yes (Ch. 11)
3-5	Pers./Soc./Think	09	Essay about emotions, "What Hits Me"	
3-5	Pers./Soc./Think	10-11	Goal setting: New Year's resolutions (2 pp.)	yes (Chs. 10, 12)
3-5	Pers./Soc./Think	12	Creativity task, "What can this be?"	
3-5	Pers./Soc./Think	13	Mother's Day card to step-mother	
3-5	Pers./Soc./Think	14	Song of myself ("I am Shea...")	
3-5	Pers./Soc./Think	15	Procedure, "How to make a new friend"	yes (Ch. 3)
3-5	Pers./Soc./Think	16-17	Story, "My Tooth"	
3-5	Pers./Soc./Think	18	Picture of sock puppets with emotions	

3-5	Pers./Soc./Think	19	Ceramic family	
3-5	Pers./Soc./Think	20	Picture of child in street with cars	
3-5	Pers./Soc./Think	21	Diary entry about physical abuse	
3-5	Pers./Soc./Think	22	Cartoon showing argument and resolution	
3-5	Pers./Soc./Think	23	Picture of boys in lunch line	
3-5	Pers./Soc./Think	24	Picture of children on playground	
3-5	Pers./Soc./Think	25	Story about getting stitches	
3-5	Pers./Soc./Think	26	Writing about friend, "Adventure Island"	
3-5	Pers./Soc./Think	27	Melanie's drawing of herself and teacher	yes (Ch. 14)
3-5	Pers./Soc./Think	28	Painting of child celebrating snowfall	
3-5	Pers./Soc./Think	29	Teacher handout, "My Broad Goals"	yes (Ch. 14)
3-5	Teacher Artifact	01	Assessment for general music	yes (Chs. 13, 16)
3-5	Teacher Artifact	02	Rubric for watercolor collage	yes (Ch. 16)
3-5	Teacher Artifact	04	Teacher handout, "My Broad Goals"	yes (Ch. 14)
6-8	Math	01	Analysis of math errors (see problem #40)	
6-8	Math	02	"Math Grade Log" (self-monitoring)	
6-8	Math	03	Test on fractions, decimals, percents	
6-8	Lang. Arts	01	Poem "Roger's Life"	
6-8	Lang. Arts	02	Poem "Dance of the Owls"	
6-8	Lang. Arts	03	Self-reflection, "I am like a stream"	
6-8	Lang. Arts	04	Descriptive prose, "Sadness"	
6-8	Lang. Arts	07	Story with spelling words, "Ghost of Count..."	yes (Ch. 4)
6-8	Lang. Arts	08	Limerick, "There once was a turkey..."	
6-8	Science	01	Exam on weather unit	yes (Chs. 15, 16)
6-8	Science	02-04	Lab report on animal and plant cells (3 pp.)	
6-8	Science	05	Drawing and description of shark	
6-8	Science	06	Drawing and description of coral polyps	
6-8	Science	07	Drawing and description of brain coral	
6-8	Science	08	Reaction paper about "variables station"	yes (Ch. 1)
6-8	Social Studies	01	Graphic notes, "Aparteid S. Africa"	
6-8	Social Studies	02	Note-taking, "South Africa"	
6-8	Social Studies	03-07	"Ancient Adventures of Sarah McBear" (5 pp.)	
6-8	Social Studies	08	Essay about Oklahoma City bombing	yes (Ch. 11)
6-8	Social Studies	09	Essay about origins of U.S. (8th grader))	yes (Ch. 2)
6-8	Social Studies	10	Essay about origins of U.S. (6th grader)	yes (Ch. 2)
6-8	Social Studies	11	Colonial village, "Colonial Village Setup"	yes (Ch. 4)
6-8	Social Studies	12	Exam on colonial America	yes (Chs. 15, 16)
6-8	Social Studies	13	Colonial village, "Faith Village"	yes (Ch. 4)
6-8	Social Studies	14-15	Campaign and election 2000 (2 pp.)	
6-8	Social Studies	16	Map of Loveland, CO (7th grader)	yes (Ch. 2)
6-8	Art & Music	01	Myra's drawing of herself and teacher	
6-8	Art & Music	02	Boys running to play baseball	
6-8	Art & Music	03	Three-dimensional spheres	
6-8	Art & Music	04	Three-dimensional jars	
6-8	Art & Music	05	Colonial village, "Colonial Village Setup"	yes (Ch. 4)
6-8	Art & Music	06	Picture of boy pushing jar of buttons	
6-8	Art & Music	07	Picture of urban neighborhood	
6-8	Art & Music	08-09	Description and drawing of Holocaust (2 pp.)	
6-8	Art & Music	10	Picture of girl looking in mirror	
6-8	Art & Music	11	Picture of boy's extended neighborhood	
6-8	Art & Music	12	Illustration of favorite activities	
6-8	Art & Music	13	Drawings of different emotions (age 13)	
6-8	Art & Music	14	Colonial village, "Faith Village"	yes (Ch. 4)

6-8	Art & Music	15	Map of Loveland, CO (7th grader)	yes (Ch. 2)
6-8	Pers./Soc./Think	01	Description, "Excitement"	
6-8	Pers./Soc./Think	02	Note-taking, "South Africa"	
6-8	Pers./Soc./Think	03	Descriptive prose, "Sadness"	
6-8	Pers./Soc./Think	04	Self-reflection, "I am like a stream"	
6-8	Pers./Soc./Think	05	Note-taking about Emily Dickinson	
6-8	Pers./Soc./Think	06	Essay about Oklahoma City bombing	yes (Ch. 11)
6-8	Pers./Soc./Think	07	Analysis of math errors (see problem #40)	
6-8	Pers./Soc./Think	08	Pictures of healthy and unhealthy girls	
6-8	Pers./Soc./Think	09	Boys running to play baseball	
6-8	Pers./Soc./Think	10	Picture of boy pushing jar of buttons	
6-8	Pers./Soc./Think	11	Picture of urban neighborhood	
6-8	Pers./Soc./Think	12-13	Description and drawing of Holocaust (2 pp.)	
6-8	Pers./Soc./Think	15	Picture of boy's extended neighborhood	
6-8	Pers./Soc./Think	16	Illustration of favorite activities	
6-8	Pers./Soc./Think	17	Myra's drawing of herself and teacher	.
6-8	Pers./Soc./Think	18	Drawing of "Funky Rap Master"	yes (Ch. 3)
6-8	Pers./Soc./Think	19	Note-taking hints	yes (Ch. 8)
6-8	Pers./Soc./Think	20	Essay about drug awareness camp	
6-8	Pers./Soc./Think	21-22	Questions about friends and friendship (2 pp.)	yes (Ch. 3)
6-8	Pers./Soc./Think	23	Drawings of different emotions (age 13)	
6-8	Pers./Soc./Think	24	Teacher handout, "Adolescent Development"	yes (Ch. 14)
6-8	Pers./Soc./Think	25	Health goals	yes (Ch. 12)
6-8	Pers./Soc./Think	29	Essay, "My Strengths..."	yes (Ch. 3)
6-8	Teacher Artifact	01	Exam on weather unit	yes (Chs. 15, 16)
6-8	Teacher Artifact	02	Exam on colonial America	yes (Chs. 15, 16)
6-8	Teacher Artifact.	03	Teacher handout, "Adolescent Development"	yes (Ch. 14)
9-12	Lang. Arts	01-03	Illustration of Paul Dunbar's "The Mask" (3 pp.)	yes (Ch. 3)
9-12	Lang. Arts	04	Diary entry about aggression at school	
9-12	Lang. Arts	06-08	Self-assessment of "Killing Plants" paper	yes (Ch. 16)
9-12	Art & Music	01	Three-dimensional hallway	
9-12	Art & Music	02	Cartoon of fish rowing upside-down	yes (Ch. 2)
9-12	Art & Music	05	Picture of self (depicted as a soda can) in cage	
9-12	Art & Music	07	Wall mural, "Saturday in Jamaica Plain"	yes (Ch. 10)
9-12	Art & Music	08	Wall mural of female basketball team	
9-12	Pers./Soc./Think	01	Cartoon of fish rowing upside-down	yes (Ch. 2)
9-12	Pers./Soc./Think	04	Picture of self (depicted as a soda can) in cage	
9-12	Pers./Soc./Think	05	Wall mural, "Saturday in Jamaica Plain"	yes (Ch. 10)
9-12	Pers./Soc./Think	07	Wall mural of female basketball team	
9-12	Pers./Soc./Think	08	Diary entry about aggression at school	
9-12	Teacher Artifact	01-02	"Common Standards" for high school	yes (Ch. 13)

USING THE *EDUCATOR LEARNING CENTER*

An unprecedented collaboration between Merrill Education and the Association of Supervision and Curriculum Development (ASCD) has produced an online library of resources for instructors and students. Known as the **Educator Learning Center**, this Website currently includes:

- **Articles from *Educational Leadership*:** More than 600 articles from the ASCD journal *Educational Leadership*. This journal is widely known for its readable and practical articles for practicing teachers and administrators.

- **Case studies:** More than 90 case studies are available for classroom discussion and analysis.

- **Strategies and lesson plans:** Numerous instructional strategies and lesson plans from key Merrill titles are categorized by content area and age range to provide hands-on resources for teachers.

- **Multimedia resources:** Simulations, tutorials, and videos from various Merrill ancillary materials are available for use on the Website.

You can find the *Educator Learning Center* at **www.educatorlearningcenter.com**. By clicking on "Demo," you can get a sample of what the Website has to offer.

The *Instructor's Manual* identifies items on the *Educator Learning Center* that may be relevant to each chapter in the textbook, but keep in mind that additional content will be added to the Website on a regular basis. Therefore, I encourage you to explore the Website periodically for additional items that might be useful.

Organization of the *Educator Learning Center*

The items contained in the *Educator Learning Center* are organized in three ways:
- By topic (including subtopics within each of two more general topics, "Classroom Processes" and "Administration and Curriculum Development")
- By subject (math, reading and language arts, social studies, science)
- By grade level (early childhood, primary, middle, secondary)

When I identify specific items in the *Instructor's Manual,* my directions for finding a particular item involve going first to the topic <u>Classroom Processes</u> and then to one of six subtopics:

- Instructional methods
- Diverse populations
- Assessment
- Classroom management
- Technology
- Refining your practice

Once you click on any one of the subtopics just listed, you will find a new menu bar that allows you to find the following items relevant to that subtopic:

1. Articles
2. Strategies
3. Multimedia
4. Case studies

Gaining Unlimited Use of the *Educator Learning Center*

Students can get a free four-month subscription to the *Educator Learning Center* when they purchase a Merrill Education textbook, and instructors have a year-long subscription. To obtain pass codes for yourself and your students, let your Merrill/Prentice Hall sales representative know that you and your students want to spend some time in this library, and your representative will give you a special ISBN to give your bookstore when you order your textbooks. (If you do not know who your local Merrill/Prentice Hall representative is, visit www.prenhall.com and click on "Find your PH rep" on the top menu bar.)

USING *SIMULATIONS IN EDUCATIONAL PSYCHOLOGY*

Accompanying each copy of *Educational Psychology: Developing Learners* is a compact disk, *Simulations in Educational Psychology*. The CD allows students to participate in several "virtual" activities, puts these simulations in a theoretical context, and helps students draw implications for educational practice. The simulations include relevant video clips of students and teachers in K-12 classrooms. An optional "Educational Research" track connected with four of the simulations also allows students to explore research and read a journal article or book chapter related to the topic in question. Each simulation is designed to stand on its own and be self-explanatory.

A CD icon appears in the margin of a textbook page whenever one of the simulations relates to chapter content. The *Study Guide and Reader* also directs students to the simulations when appropriate.

In the "Transparency Masters" section at the end of this manual, you can find a transparency master that lists the five simulations and presents preliminary instructions for using the CD. You can use the transparency to assist you as you describe the CD to your students.

The five simulations are briefly described on this and the following page. Each one is described in greater detail in the subsequent sections.

The Pendulum Experiment
This simulation lets students "experiment" with a virtual pendulum. They can manipulate one or more of three variables (height of release, weight, and length), and the computer keeps an ongoing record of the oscillation rates that result. Following the student's experiments is an explanation of the role that the ability to separate and control variables plays in Piaget's theory of cognitive development, and implications for classroom practice are considered. The simulation relates to content in Chapter 2 and "Learning in the Content Areas."

Assessing Moral Reasoning
This simulation first presents a moral dilemma that a teacher might face and asks students to decide what the teacher should do and why. It then describes Kohlberg's theory of moral development and illustrates how people at different stages might respond to Kohlberg's classic "Heinz dilemma." Students become "Apprentice Raters" who analyze responses to several moral dilemmas with respect to the moral reasoning reflected. Later, students consider strategies for promoting moral development in the classroom. The simulation relates to content in Chapter 3.

Bartlett's Ghosts
This simulation is based on studies conducted by F. C. Bartlett in 1932. Students read Bartlett's classic story "War of the Ghosts" and recall what they can remember of the story. They compare their own version against the original and record their omissions, transformations, and additions.

Also included are discussions of schema theory and implications for classroom practice. The simulation relates to content in Chapter 7.

Intuitive Physics

Students are asked to predict the path that an object will take when it is (a) pushed over the edge of a cliff, (b) carried along a conveyor belt and reaches the end of the belt, and (c) carried by a flying airplane and then released. Students receive feedback about the path that the object will actually take, and relevant principles of physics are described. The resilience of student misconceptions is discussed, and recommendations for promoting conceptual change are presented. The simulation relates to content in Chapters 7 and 8 and "Learning in the Content Areas."

Assessment in the Balance

Students gain practice in analyzing children's responses to both performance assessment and paper-pencil assessment tasks. They learn how to draw conclusions about children's mental models from responses to a variety of beam balance problems. They then consider the kinds of information they can glean from three classroom artifacts: a kindergartner's attempt to write the numbers 1-20, a fourth grader's science lab report, and a seventh grader's English essay. The simulation relates to content in Chapters 8 and 16.

THE PENDULUM EXPERIMENT

Brief Description: The simulation lets students conduct virtual "experiments" with a pendulum. They can manipulate one or more of three variables (height of release, weight, and length), and the computer keeps an ongoing record of the oscillation rates that result. Following such experimentation is a description of Piaget's preoperational, concrete operational, and formal operational stages, and educational implications of Piaget's theory are presented. Later, three video clips show four seventh graders experimenting with and reasoning about a pendulum's swing, and three additional video clips show their teacher's strategies for encouraging separation and control of variables. An optional "Educational Research" track introduces basic concepts and types of educational research and presents a research article concerning the effects of prior knowledge on children's ability to separate and control variables. Students can print out their responses and bring them to class.

Relevant Chapters: Chapter 2 and "Learning in the Content Areas"

Detailed Description

The simulation has five components, as follows:

Introduction (Frames 1-3). The nature of a pendulum problem is described, and the pendulum problem is introduced in the form of the question *What characteristics of a pendulum determine how fast it swings?* Students are asked to type several hypotheses regarding variables that might influence a pendulum's oscillation rate. Three potential variables are then identified: the height of release, weight, and length.

Laboratory (Frame 4). In the "laboratory" (see Figure 1), students can experiment with height, weight, and/or length and observe the effects of these variables on oscillation rate. They are instructed to:

1. <u>Form your hypothesis.</u> They select one or more of the three variables they will be testing.
2. <u>Design your experiment.</u> They select a level for each variable (*height* = low, medium, or high; *weight* = 25, 50, or 100 grams; *length* = 5, 10, or 15 inches).
3. <u>Run your experiment.</u> They click on the "Run" button and watch the pendulum swing. The oscillation rate appears near the bottom of the screen.
4. <u>Analyze your results.</u> The selected levels for the three variables and the resulting oscillation rate are displayed in a table along with the results of any previous experiments.

Students can conduct as many experiments as they wish before proceeding to the next frame.

Reflection and debrief (Frames 5-6). Students examine the results of their experiments and then reflect on what they were thinking as they conducted each one. They describe their thoughts in a textbox on the computer screen (see Figure 2). After they enter their response, the following text appears:

> Did you test each hypothesis in a systematic fashion? A student capable of formal operational thinking separates and controls variables, testing one at a time while holding all others constant. For example, if you were testing the hypothesis that weight makes a difference, you might have tried different weights while keeping constant the length of

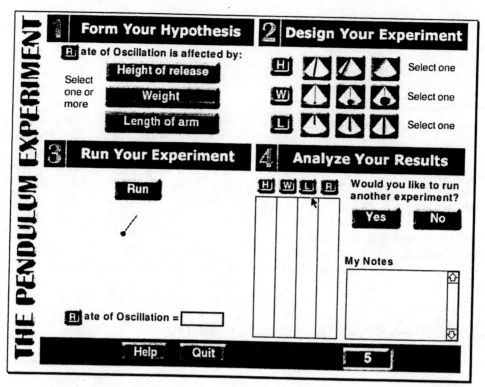

Figure 1. The pendulum "laboratory"

the arm and the height of release. Similarly, if you hypothesized that the length of the arm was a critical factor, you might have varied the length of the arm while continuing to use the same weight and releasing the pendulum from the same height. If you carefully separated and controlled the variables that you considered, then you would have come to the correct conclusion: Only length affects a pendulum's rate of oscillation.

Educational implications (Frames 7-21). In a frame entitled "Opportunities for Learning," students are asked to choose either an "Educational Psychology" track or an "Educational Research" track. When they click on the "Educational Psychology" button, they read about the role that separation and control of variables plays in Piaget's formal operations stage. A table contrasts various aspects of concrete and formal operational thought (the table is similar to one in Chapter 2 of the textbook but also includes combinatorial thought). Students then observe three video clips from Mr. Scott Sowell's seventh-grade science class, where a group of four children is conducting experiments with a pendulum.

1. After the group has conducted several experiments, Mr. Sowell stops by and asks how they are doing. Marina tells him, 'We found out that the shorter it is and the heavier it is, the faster it goes."

2. After some coaching by Mr. Sowell, the group conducts another test. Once the test is completed, Paige, says, "Now compare this test to the second test. It's the same height and the same weight. It's just the length that's different."

3. Still later in the activity, a student explains to Mr. Sowell that they found that "The height was . . . higher but the weight was lower, so it's the same thing."

Students are asked to determine whether the children are exhibiting concrete operational or formal operational thought in each case.

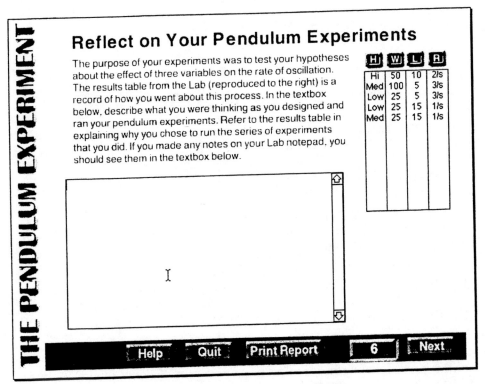

Figure 2. Reflection frame in which a student considers the results of his or her experiments

Students are then asked to consider Mr. Sowell's teaching strategies in three situations:

1. How he responds when Marina says, "The shorter it is and the heavier it is, the faster it goes."
2. How he introduces and scaffolds the pendulum activity at the beginning of class
3. How he nudges the children toward more sophisticated reasoning during the course of their experimentation

Educational research (Frames 22-56). Following the discussion of educational implications, students are given the choice either to exit the program or to pursue the "Educational Research" track. If the "Educational Research" track is selected, students (a) read a series of frames that discuss basic concepts in educational research (*variable, independent variable, dependent variable, hypothesis*) and several types of research (*historical, qualitative, descriptive, correlational, causal-comparative, experimental*); and (b) read and analyze a research article related to children's ability to separate and control variables:

Pulos, S., & Linn, M. C. (1981). Generality of the controlling variables scheme in early adolescence. *Journal of Early Adolescence, 1,* 36-37.

Students are then asked to respond to the following:

1. State the purpose of the study.
2. What is the independent variable?
3. What is the dependent variable?
4. Describe the sample used.
5. Describe the procedures.
6. Describe the method of analysis.
7. Describe the results of the study.

8. State the major conclusions.
9. Classify the study—what type of study is it?

Using the Simulation with Chapter 2 or "Learning in the Content Areas"

When you assign the simulation: Tell your students that the simulation provides an alternative to the Experiencing Firsthand exercise "Pendulum Problem" in Chapter 2. Also tell students that when they reach the frame entitled "Opportunities for Learning," they should click on the "Educational Psychology" button for a discussion of educational implications. In addition, give them *one* of the following instructions:

1. *(If your instructional objectives do not include the understanding and/or analysis of psychological and educational research)* "When you reach the frame entitled 'Further Exploration,' click the 'Quit' button to exit the program."

2. *(If you want to introduce basic concepts in research and basic categories of research studies)* "When you reach the frame entitled 'Further Exploration,' click the 'Educational Research' button to read a short discussion about concepts and categories related to educational research. When you reach the frame 'Reading the Article,' click the 'Quit' button to exit the program."

3. *(If your students have had some background in reading and analyzing research reports)* "When you reach the frame entitled 'Further Exploration,' click the 'Educational Research' button to read a brief review of basic concepts in educational research. Then read and analyze the research article by Pulos and Linn about young adolescents' ability to separate and control variables in different contexts." (Note: Depending on the degree of students' knowledge about research methods, you may want them to respond only to a subset of the nine questions the CD poses about the article.)

If all students have access to a computer printer, you might also ask that they click the "Print Report" button before clicking the "Quit" button and bring their report to the next class session.

After students have completed the simulation: You might ask questions such as these:

- How effectively did you separate and control variables? Did you consistently hold two of the variables constant while testing the effects of the third? Or did you sometimes confound two or more variables?

- Do you think the textbook's discussion of the importance of separating and controlling variables influenced the experimental procedure you used?

- What are some possible reasons why children in the elementary grades often fail to separate and control variables?

- In the "Educational Implications" section, did you analyze any of the scenarios differently than the expert did? If so, how were your analyses different?

ASSESSING MORAL REASONING

Brief Description: The simulation presents several moral dilemmas and shows how people's responses reflect reasoning at different stages in Kohlberg's theory of moral development. Also included are a discussion of instructional strategies for promoting moral development, three video clips depicting classrooms where moral issues are raised, and an optional "Educational Research" track (in which alternative approaches to assessing moral reasoning are described and a relevant research article is presented). Students can print out their responses and bring them to class.

Relevant Chapter: Chapter 3

Detailed Description

The simulation has four components, as follows:

Introduction (Frames 1-3). The following situation is presented to illustrate a *moral dilemma*:

> Ms. Cole, an outstanding veteran social studies teacher, specializes in constitutional issues and has raised concerns about her school district's drug testing policy. She has always told her students to follow their conscience when faced with unjust laws. She has recently become the target of a police search—a police dog is alleged to have smelled marijuana in the teacher's car ashtray. Ms. Cole is required to take a mandatory drug test within 48 hours. Since she believes the policy is unconstitutional, she must decide whether to practice what she preaches and refuse to take the drug test or to ignore her conscience and submit to the test. Ms. Cole is one year away from retirement and will lose her job and pension if she refuses to take the test.
>
> Should the teacher take the drug test? Explain why you think the teacher should or should not take the drug test.

The nature of moral dilemmas is described, and Kohlberg's stage theory of moral reasoning is introduced.

Assessment lab (Frames 4-16). Kohlberg's classic "Heinz dilemma" (also found in an Experiencing Firsthand exercise in Chapter 3) is presented, and nine responses are shown to illustrate reasoning at different stages of moral development. (Kohlberg's Stage 6 is omitted due to its lack of empirical support.) Students then act as "Apprentice Raters" to evaluate various responses to three other dilemmas, including the "drug test" dilemma presented above and these "cheating" and "software copying" dilemmas:

> Bruce finds out that some of his classmates obtained the answers to an exam before taking it. He [should/should not] report the cheating because....

> Mr. Collins is told about some software that will help several of his students improve their understanding of an important math concept. The school administration claims there is no money for the software, even considering the software company's educational discount. The person who told Mr. Collins about the software offers to make him an illegal copy for him to use in his classroom. He [should/should not] accept the free software because....

After identifying the stages that various responses reflect, students return to their own response to the drug test dilemma. (Students are assured that their response to a single dilemma is not necessarily an indication of their overall level of moral reasoning.)

Educational implications (Frames 17-24). In the "Educational Psychology" track, several strategies for promoting moral development are presented. Students then view three video clips of classrooms in actions and are asked to consider how a teacher either is promoting or might promote moral development:

1. On the first day of school, a second-grade teacher and her students discuss rules for classroom behavior.

2. A high school history teacher explains why in 1956, government officials in South Vietnam decided not to hold the free elections called for by the Geneva Accords.

3. A high school English teacher asks students to reflect on two different characters' perspectives in Nathaniel Hawthorne's *The Scarlet Letter*.

Educational research (Frames 25-70). Following the discussion of educational implications, students are given the choice either to exit the program or to pursue the "Educational Research" track. If the "Educational Research" track is selected, students (a) read about alternative approaches to assessing moral reasoning and have a firsthand experience with one approach, and (b) read and analyze a research article related to assessment of moral reasoning:

Basinger, K. S., Gibbs, J. C., & Fuller, D. (1995). Context and the measurement of moral judgment. *International Journal of Behavioral Development, 18,* 537-556.

Students are then asked to respond to the following:

1. State the purpose of the study.
2. What is the independent variable?
3. What is the dependent variable?
4. Describe the sample used.
5. Describe the procedures.
6. Describe the method of analysis.
7. Describe the results of the study.
8. State the major conclusions.
9. Classify the study—what type of study is it?

Using the Simulation with Chapter 3

When you assign the simulation: Tell your students that the simulation provides additional information and practice related to Kohlberg's stages of moral reasoning. Also tell them that when they reach the frame entitled "Opportunities for Learning," they should click on the "Educational Psychology" button for a discussion of educational implications; encourage them to use the "Compare!" button to compare their responses with those that an expert might make. In addition, give them *one* of the following instructions:

1. *(If students have had little or no previous experience reading research articles, and if you want to limit the exercise to Kohlberg's approach to assessing moral reasoning)* "When you reach the frame entitled 'Further Exploration,' click the 'Quit' button to exit the program."

2. *(If students have had little or no previous experience reading research articles, and if you want students to explore alternative ways of assessing moral reasoning)* "When you reach the frame entitled 'Further Exploration,' click the 'Educational Research' button to learn about alternative ways of assessing moral reasoning. When you reach the frame 'Reading the Article,' click the 'Quit' button to exit the program."

3. *(If your students have had some background in reading and analyzing research reports)* "When you reach the frame entitled 'Further Exploration,' click the 'Educational Research' button to learn about alternative ways of assessing moral reasoning and to read and analyze an article about an alternative assessment method." (Note: Depending on the degree of students' knowledge about research methods, you may want them to respond only to a subset of the nine questions the CD poses about the article.)

If all students have access to a computer printer, you might also ask that they click the "Print Report" button before clicking the "Quit" button and bring their report to the next class session.

After students have completed the simulation: You might ask questions such as these:

- Did you code any of the responses to the dilemmas differently than the expert did? If so, what was your rationale?

- What are the advantages and disadvantages of assessing moral development in the way that Kohlberg did?

- In what other ways might researchers assess moral development?

- What opportunities might you have to promote moral development in your own classrooms?

BARTLETT'S GHOSTS

Brief Description: This simulation is based loosely on studies that Frederic C. Bartlett described in his classic 1932 book *Remembering: A Study in Experimental and Social Psychology* (Cambridge University Press). Students read Bartlett's "War of the Ghosts" and type what they can remember of the story. They compare their recalled version with the original and identify their omissions, transformations, and additions. Also included in the activity are a brief theoretical discussion of schema theory, implications for classroom practice, analysis of three classroom video clips, and an optional "Educational Research" track (in which students analyze responses that Bartlett's subjects gave and read Bransford and Johnson's classic 1972 research article dealing with constructive processes). Students can print out their responses and bring them to class.

Relevant Chapter: Chapter 7

Detailed Description

The simulation has four components, as follows:

"War of the Ghosts" (Frames 1-4). As students begin the activity, they read Bartlett's story "War of the Ghosts" (this story also appears in an Experiencing Firsthand exercise in Chapter 7 of the textbook). They are then asked to type as much of the story as they can remember. After their recall, they are given the following introduction to Bartlett's experiment:

> Bartlett first ran this experiment in 1913. After participants wrote their versions of the "War of the Ghosts," he compared them to the original story. As you would expect, participants' versions omitted, changed, or added details.

> But what was novel about Bartlett's approach was his focus on what he called the "effort after meaning," rather than on the accuracy of recall. He theorized that an individual's mental "schemas"—organized bodies of knowledge about specific objects and events—would influence what was remembered. Details that did not fit into a person's schemas would be forgotten or transformed into something more familiar. People might add details not in the original because their existing schemas, activated by reading the story, provided details consistent with the meaning of the story.

> Of course, different people read different meanings into the story, so Bartlett asked participants to share some of their thoughts after they completed the recall task. He then attempted to explain the omissions, transformations, and additions based on each individual's mental schemas.

Analysis lab (Frames 5-7). Students enter an "Analysis Lab" in which they analyze their own stories for omissions, transformations, and additions (see Figure 3). Following their analysis, they read about how their errors may reflect the constructive nature of memory and about how schemas may have played a role in their constructions.

Educational implications (Frames 8-14). In a frame entitled "Opportunities for Learning," students are asked to choose either an "Educational Psychology" track or an "Educational Research" track. When they click on the "Educational Psychology" button, they proceed to a

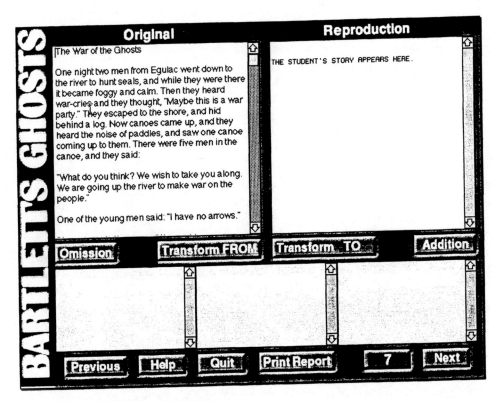

Figure 3. The "Analysis Lab"

discussion of educational implications of schema theory and are asked to reflect on and analyze the following scenario:

> Mr. Goldberg's class has already learned that insects have three body parts and six legs. Then he says, "Let's take a look at a picture of a wasp. See? It has all the parts that insects have, so it must be an insect." Given what you have just learned, is this an effective strategy?

After they have addressed this scenario, they apply what they have learned about the effects of prior knowledge (e.g., schemas and personal theories) as they watch video clips of a high school chemistry lesson, an elementary school math lesson, and a middle school group working on reading and study skills.

Educational research (Frames 15-49). Following the discussion of educational implications and video clip analyses, students are given the choice either to exit the program or to pursue the "Educational Research" track. If the "Educational Research" track is selected, students are asked to (a) analyze two stories that Bartlett's original subjects produced and (b) read and analyze a research article related to knowledge construction:

> Bransford, J. D., & Johnson, M. K. (1972). Contextual prerequisites for understanding: Some investigations of comprehension and recall. *Journal of Verbal Learning and Verbal Behavior, 11,* 717-726.

Students are then asked to respond to the following:

1. State the purpose of the study.
2. What is the independent variable?
3. What is the dependent variable?
4. Describe the sample used.
5. Describe the procedures.

6. Describe the method of analysis.
7. Describe the results of the study.
8. State the major conclusions.
9. Classify the study—what type of study is it?

Using the Simulation with Chapter 7

When you assign the simulation: Tell your students that the simulation is a more interactive version of the Experiencing Firsthand exercise "The War of the Ghosts" in Chapter 7. Also tell them that when they reach the frame entitled "Opportunities for Learning," they should click on the "Educational Psychology" button for a discussion of educational implications. In addition, give them *one* of the following instructions:

1. *(If students have had little or no previous experience reading research articles, and if you want to limit the exercise to an analysis of students' own responses)* "When you reach the frame entitled 'Further Exploration,' click the 'Quit' button to exit the program."

2. *(If students have had little or no previous experience reading research articles, and if you want students to analyze the responses of Bartlett's subjects)* "When you reach the frame entitled 'Further Exploration,' click the 'Educational Research' button to analyze two stories that Bartlett's subjects recalled. When you reach the frame 'Reading the Article,' click the 'Quit' button to exit the program."

3. *(If your students have had some background in reading and analyzing research reports)* "When you reach the frame entitled 'Further Exploration,' click the 'Educational Research' button to analyze two stories that Bartlett's subjects recalled and to read and analyze Bransford and Johnson's classic article on constructive processes in learning and memory." (Note: Depending on the degree of students' knowledge about research methods, you may want them to respond only to a subset of the nine questions the CD poses about the article.)

If all students have access to a computer printer, you might also ask that they click the "Print Report" button before clicking the "Quit" button and bring their report to the next class session.

After students have completed the simulation: You might ask one or more of the following questions:

• What kinds of errors did you make in recalled the story?

• Can you explain your errors in terms of certain schemas you might have?

• Bartlett asked many of his students to recall the story several weeks or months after they had first heard it? How might such a lengthy time lapse influence the quality of their recall?

• In the "Educational Implications" section, did you analyze any of the scenarios differently than the expert did? If so, how were your analyses different?

INTUITIVE PHYSICS

Brief Description: The simulation is based on Michael McCloskey's 1983 article in *Scientific American* ("Intuitive Physics," *248*(4), pp. 122-130). Students are asked to predict the path that an object will take when it is (a) pushed over the edge of a cliff, (b) carried along a conveyor belt and reaches the end of the belt, and (c) carried by a flying airplane and then released. Students receive feedback about the path that the object will actually take in each instance, and they learn relevant principles of physics. The resilience of student misconceptions is discussed, recommendations for promoting conceptual change are offered, and three video clips of a fourth grader whose reasoning reflects misconceptions are presented. An optional "Educational Research" track discusses how research about misconceptions can guide educational practice and includes a book chapter in which McCloskey describes his research.

Relevant Chapters: Chapters 7 and 8 and "Learning in the Content Areas"

Detailed Description

The simulation has five components, as follows:

Identifying beliefs about motion (Frames 1-6). Students see a ball after it has been pushed toward the edge of a cliff and are asked to predict the direction the ball will fall once it reaches the cliff; after they make their prediction, an animated depiction of the correct path appears. Students are then given this situation:

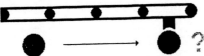

A ball is attached to a conveyor belt by an electromagnet. When the ball reaches the edge of the cliff, the magnet is turned off, releasing the ball. Which path will the ball take on the way down?

Once again, after students make a prediction, an animated depiction of the correct path (a path identical to that of the ball pushed over the cliff) appears. Students are asked, "What do these two problems have in common?" Sir Isaac Newton's theories on gravity and motion are described, as follows:

In 1687, Sir Isaac Newton published his theories on gravity and motion. Three hundred years later, we still rely on his theories to calculate the motion of objects. The power of a theory is its ability to ignore irrelevant features and focus on underlying principles. When you apply Newton's theory to these two problems, you ignore how the ball was put into motion. All that matters is that an object continues to move in a straight line unless acted upon by external forces, such as gravity and air resistance. Whether the ball was pushed, shot from a cannon, carried by a conveyor belt or a person makes no difference. Since the Newtonian view is not distracted by this irrelevant aspect of the two problems, it results in the same (correct) prediction each time. Two identical objects traveling at the same speed will trace the same path (falling to the earth due to the influence of gravity and air resistance), regardless of how they achieved that speed.

Prior to Newton, scientists believed that a person throwing an object imparted a force, often called an "impetus," that stayed with the object even after it left the grasp of the thrower. Someone holding an impetus view may believe that a force, or impetus, is imparted to the pushed or propelled ball but NOT the carried ball, and therefore, predict different paths for the cliff and the conveyor situations.

Students learn that the "impetus" misconception is common even among students who have studied physics in high school or college; they also read examples of student statements that reflect the misconception.

Transfer task (Frame 7). Students are given the following situation:

A C.A.R.E. package is dropped from a moving airplane. Which path will the package take on the way down?

After students make a prediction, the correct answer—a path identical to that in the cliff and conveyor problems—is shown in an animated fashion.

Debrief (Frames 8-11). The persistence of student misconceptions is discussed, and several teaching strategies for addressing students' misconceptions are described.

Educational implications (Frames 12-18). In the "Educational Psychology" track, principles related to conceptual change are presented and discussed. Students are then asked to analyze three video clips in which a fourth grader shows misconceptions in her reasoning about balance scale problems.

Educational research (Frames 19-66). Following the discussion of educational implications, students are given the choice either to exit the program or to pursue the "Educational Research" track. If the "Educational Research" track is selected, students (a) read a brief passage about how research about misconceptions can guide teaching practice, and (b) read and analyze a book chapter about student misconceptions:

> McCloskey, M. (1983). Naive theories of motion. In D. Gentner & A. L. Stevens (Eds.), *Mental models*. Hillsdale, NJ: Erlbaum.

Students are then asked to respond to the following:

1. State the purpose of the study.
2. What is the independent variable?
3. What is the dependent variable?
4. Describe the sample used.
5. Describe the procedures.
6. Describe the method of analysis.
7. Describe the results of the study.
8. State the major conclusions.
9. Classify the study—what type of study is it?

Using the Simulation with Chapter 7, Chapter 8, or "Learning in the Content Areas"

When you assign the simulation: Tell your students that the simulation explores the nature of student beliefs and misconceptions related to the motion of objects, as well as the extent to which such beliefs and misconceptions may transfer from one situation to another. Also tell them that when they reach the frame entitled "Opportunities for Learning," they should click on the "Educational Psychology" button for a discussion of educational implications; encourage them to use the "Compare!" button to compare their teaching strategies to those that an expert might recommend. In addition, give them *one* of the following instructions:

1. *(If you do not want students to explore the role that research plays in our knowledge about student misconceptions)* "When you reach the frame entitled 'Further Exploration,' click the 'Quit' button to exit the program."

2. *(If students have had little or no previous experience reading research articles, but you want them to read a short description of how research can inform educational practice)* "When you reach the frame entitled 'Further Exploration,' click the 'Educational Research' button to read a frame entitled 'Benefits of Research.' When you reach the frame 'Reading the Article,' click the 'Quit' button to exit the program."

3. *(If your students have had some background in reading and analyzing research reports)* "When you reach the frame entitled 'Further Exploration,' click the 'Educational Research' button to read a book chapter in which Michael McCloskey describes his research related to students' misconceptions about objects in motion." (Note: Depending on the degree of students' knowledge about research methods, you may want them to respond only to a subset of the nine questions the CD poses about the article.)

If all students have access to a computer printer, you might also ask that they click the "Print Report" button before clicking the "Quit" button and bring their report to the next class session.

After students have completed the simulation: You might ask questions such as these:

- Did you predict the same path for the cliff, conveyor, and airplane problems? If not, why not?

- What everyday experiences seem to contradict Newton's laws of motion?

- *(If students have read or are reading Chapter 8)* Did you successfully transfer what you learned about the cliff and conveyor situations to the airplane problem? If so, why? If not, why not?

- *(If students have read or are reading Chapter 8)* Why might some students have difficulty transferring what they learn in a physics class to the cliff, conveyor, and/or airplane problems?

ASSESSMENT IN THE BALANCE

Brief Description: The simulation allows students to examine children's reasoning about problems involving beam balances and gives them hands-on practice with both performance and paper-pencil assessment tasks. In the first part of the simulation, students construct a variety of beam balance problems and see how four different children (William, Marta, Chrys, and Ravi) solve each problem; your students' task is to form and test hypotheses about the mental model each child is using while reasoning about the problems. Later, students examine and analyze three classroom artifacts: a kindergartner's attempt to write the numbers 1-20, a fourth grader's science lab report, and a seventh grader's English essay. Finally, students are asked to reflect on the assessment activities they have completed, and general guidelines for classroom assessment are offered.

Relevant Chapters: Chapters 8 and 16

Detailed Description

The simulation has three components, as follows:

Assessment in the Balance (Frames 3-24). Students explore how teachers can make inferences about students' mental models by posing beam balance problems. The simulation proceeds through the following sequence:

Frames 3-5. The general nature of beam balance problems is described, but at this point no information about how to solve such problems is given. Students are urged to look beyond the particular answers that children give and to consider the reasoning that underlies their answers.

Frames 6-8 ("Assessment Lab"). Students see photographs of four children (William, Marta, Chrys, and Ravi) who will be responding to the problems that the students will construct. In Frame 6, students are told that they will:
1. Construct a series of balance problems that each child will solve.
2. Build a mental model of each child's understanding of a beam balance
3. Predict how each child will respond to any balance problem

In Frame 7 (see Figure 4), students place one to four weights on either side of a beam balance and then see the predictions that each of the four children makes about what the balance will do (fall to the left, fall to the right, or balance). Students can "present" as many problems to the children as they wish, and the computer keeps a running record of how the children respond in each case. In Frame 8, the computer presents additional problems to the four children, and students are asked to predict how each child will respond.

Frame 9. In the preceding Assessment Lab, many students may have discovered that they were having difficulty predicting how the children would respond to some of the problems. In this frame, they learn that three things are important for adequately assessing students' performance:

    <u>Content knowledge</u>: In our beam balance example, you yourself needed to understand how the balance works.

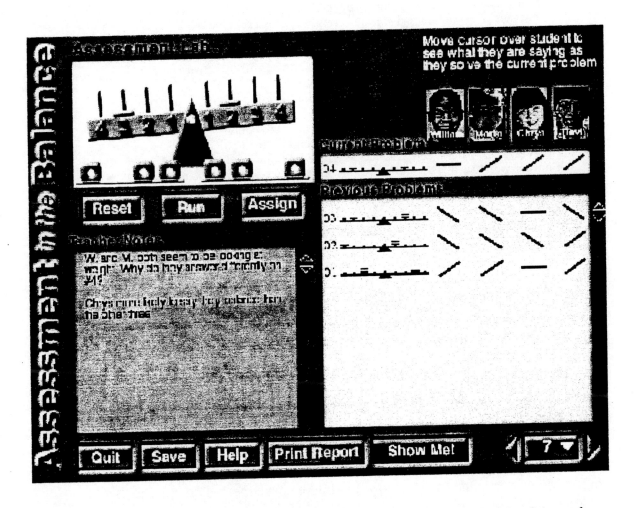

Figure 4. The "Assessment Lab." The student drags 1-4 weights to each side of the scale, pushes the "Run" button to discover whether the scale balances, and pushes the "Assign" button to learn each child's prediction. The "Reset" button allows the student to construct another problem for the children to solve.

Mental models: You needed to understand different ways in which someone can think about how the balance works.

Problem construction: You needed to be able to construct problems that would assess and differentiate the ways in which your four students came up with their answers.

Frames 10-11: These frames explain the three factors that determine whether the beam will balance: weight, distance, and torque.

Frame 12: Four possible mental models of a beam balance (based on Siegler, 1976[1]) are described:

1. Some children focus exclusively on weight.
2. Others begin to consider distance, but only under limited circumstances.

---

[1] Siegler, R. S. (1976). Three aspects of cognitive development. *Cognitive Psychology, 8,* 481-520.

3. Students who always consider distance and weight may not know what to do when distance is greater on one side and weight is greater on the other.

4. Some students know that the downward force, or "torque," on one side is equal to the weight times the distance from the fulcrum. They use this formula to compare the torque on each side and determine which side, if either, will tilt down.

Frame 13: Seven different types of beam balance problems are described and illustrated:
Balance: Weights and distances are equal.
Weight: Weight is greater on one side, distances are equal.
Distance: Distance is greater on one side, weights are equal.
Non-conflict: Weight and distance are greater on one side.
Conflict-weight: Weight and torque are greater on one side, distance is greater on the other.
Conflict-distance: Distance and torque are greater on one side, weight is greater on the other.
Conflict-balance: Weight and distance are greater on opposite sides, balancing each other out.

Using a combination of these problem types, teachers can determine which of the four mental models a particular child is using.

Frames 14-15 ("Mental Model Lab"): The four mental models are illustrated with flowcharts, and students can clearly see how, developmentally, each builds on the model that precedes it. Using each model, students make predictions for seven beam balance problems.

Frames 16-19 (""Assessment Lab II"): Students return to the Assessment Lab and try to identify the specific mental model that each of the four children (William, Marta, Chrys, and Ravi) is using.

Frames 20-23: Video clips are presented in which three children (Danielle, Maderin, and Becky) solve beam balance problems in a classroom, and students are asked to draw inferences about the children's mental models.

Frame 24: Students watch a video clip in which two children describe a beam balance problem as they see it and compare how the children have mentally represented (i.e., *encoded*) the problem.

Assessing Student Learning (Frames 25-58). Students look at the nature of assessment more generally and discover the many things they can learn about a child from any single assessment task.

Frames 25-26. Assessment is described as having many possible purposes, including these three:
- It can promote students' learning.
- It can promote the development of self-regulation skills.
- It can help teachers determine whether instructional goals have been achieved.

Frames 27-36 ("Kindergarten: Numbers"): A kindergartner (Jameel) has been asked to write the numbers 1-20. Students type notes regarding conclusions they can draw from the artifact. They are then asked if, in their assessment, they considered each of the following in their analysis:
- Knowledge of the correct order of different numbers
- Knowledge about right-left and top-bottom orientation
- Eye-hand coordination

After reexamining the artifact with these characteristics in mind, they compare their own analysis with that of an expert and are asked to reflect of why the child might have made the errors he did. They also consider how the assessment task might be used for each of the three purposes of assessment introduced in Frame 26, as well as how their own content knowledge was essential to conducting the assessment and what inferences might be drawn about Jameel's mental model of the number system.

Frames 37-49 ("Grade 4: Lab Report"): A fourth grader (Jeff) has written a lab report about his group's dissection of a cow's eye. Students read the report and draw preliminary conclusions about the child's knowledge and abilities. They are then asked if they considered each of the following in their analysis:

- Knowledge about how vision works
- Knowledge about the anatomy of the eye
- Ability to follow directions
- Written language skills
- Handwriting and/or eye-hand coordination

After reexamining the lab report with these characteristics in mind, they compare their own analysis with that of an expert and look more closely at what the report reveals about the child's knowledge of science, spelling, and sentence structure. They consider how the report might be helpful for the three purposes of assessment presented in Frame 26, and the point is made that any single assignment can allow a teacher to assess multiple abilities · simultaneously.

Frames 50-58 ("Grade 7: English essay"): A seventh grader (Christina) has written an essay to practice argumentative writing. After conducting an initial evaluation, students are asked if they considered each of the following in their analysis:

- Choice of a particular position on the issue
- Use of three reasons or sources of evidence in support of the position
- Clear, in-depth explanation of each reason or source of evidence
- Knowledge of writing mechanics (e.g., capitalization, punctuation, spelling, indentation, grammatical correctness
- Neatness
- Relationships with family
- Attitudes about homework

After reexamining the essay with these characteristics in mind, they compare their analysis with that of an expert and consider how they might use the essay for each of the three purposes of assessment identified in Frame 26.

General discussion of assessment (Frames 59-65): Students are asked to reflect on the difficulties they faced during one or more of the assessment activities. Five general principles of assessment are presented:

1. To effectively assess students' work, you yourself must have mastered the content being assessed.
2. Your judgments about a student's performance should depend on what children at different ages can reasonably be expected to do.
3. Classroom assessments must be related to instructional goals.
4. Any single assessment can simultaneously yield information about students' learning and achievement in several different areas.
5. The more relevant information an assessment yields, the better able teachers are to identify an appropriate course for future instruction.

Using the Simulation with Chapter 8

When you assign the simulation: Tell your students that the simulation provides an opportunity to explore children's reasoning processes related to beam balance problems. On the opening menu, they should click on "Assessment in the Balance." When they get to the next screen, they should sign in; they can then proceed with the activity itself by clicking on the arrow in the lower right corner of the screen. When students get to Frame 7, they should first click on the "Show Me" button to learn how to conduct the assessment lab. For purposes of Chapter 8, they should probably quit the program once they reach Frame 25. If all students have access to a computer printer, you might also ask that they click the "Print Report" button before quitting the program and bring their report to the next class session.

After students have completed the simulation: You might ask questions such as these:

- How are the *mental models* described in the simulation similar to the *personal theories* described in Chapter 7?

- Before you did the simulation, were you familiar with the concept of *torque* and how it affects a beam balance? If not, did you find yourself at a loss to interpret the children's responses the first time you completed the Assessment Lab?

- Why is it important to look not only at how students solve problems but also at how they reason about the problems?

Using the Simulation with Chapter 16

When you assign the simulation: Tell your students that the simulation provides practice in assessing both performance and paper-pencil tasks and that the entire simulation will probably take one to two hours. On the opening menu, they should click on "Assessment in the Balance." When they get to the next screen, they should sign in; they can then proceed with the activity itself by clicking on the arrow in the lower right corner of the screen. When students get to Frame 7, they should first click on the "Show Me" button to learn how to conduct the assessment lab. If all students have access to a computer printer, you might also ask that they click the "Print Report" button at the end of the program (Frame 65) and bring their report to the next class session.

After students have completed the simulation: You might ask questions such as these:

- How are the *mental models* described in the simulation similar to the *personal theories* described in Chapter 7?

- Before you did the simulation, were you familiar with the concept of *torque* and how it affects a beam balance? If not, did you find yourself at a loss to interpret the children's responses the first time you completed the Assessment Lab?

- Why is it important to look not only at how students solve problems but also at how they reason about the problems?

- What kinds of information did you glean from the kindergartner's numbers? from the fourth grader's lab report? from the seventh grader's persuasive essay? Did you notice anything that the expert did *not* notice?

- How might you use each of the three written artifacts to promote student learning? to promote self-regulation?

- Frame 59 asked you to reflect on difficulties you had in the various assessment tasks included in the simulation. What difficulties did you identify? How might you minimize such difficulties when you're conducting actual assessments in the classroom?

USING THE MERRILL VIDEOTAPES

Nine videotapes accompany *Educational Psychology: Developing Learners* and can be obtained by contacting your local Prentice Hall sales representative. Suggestions for using the videos appear in the pages that follow. The nature of each video is as follows:

A Private Universe

This video illustrates the pervasiveness of misconceptions about two scientific phenomena—the seasons of the year and the phases of the moon—not only in high school students but even in graduates and faculty members at Harvard University. One high-achieving ninth grader's explanations are portrayed in depth both before and after instruction. Although the student shows improved understanding following instruction, questions that probe into her reasoning reveal that she still holds on to some of her prior misconceptions. (18 minutes)

Double-Column Addition: A Teacher Uses Piaget's Theory

This video shows children in a second-grade class developing strategies for adding and subtracting two-digit numbers. The teacher does not directly teach such strategies; instead, she helps the children to construct their own strategies by presenting problems, asking for possible solutions, and encouraging class discussion of different approaches. The students develop a variety of creative strategies for adding and subtracting two-digit numbers, many of which reflect a true conceptual understanding of place value in two-digit numbers. (20 minutes)

Using Balance Beams in Fourth Grade

A fourth-grade teacher has students work in small groups to solve problems involving weights on a balance beam; the video focuses on the problem-solving activities and discussions of Molly, Drexel, Susie, and Tad. Later, the teacher conducts a whole-class discussion in which she has various students present and defend heir problem solutions. Following the class discussion, a college professor meets with Molly, Drexel, Susie, and Tad to present additional problems and probe their reasoning. Finally, the teacher reflects on the lesson.

Finding Area in Elementary Math

Within the context of an authentic activity (determining how much carpet will be needed to cover a portion of the classroom floor), a fifth-grade teacher has her students work in small groups to find the area of an irregular shape. She uses five "Steps in Problem Solving" to guide the activity. Periodically the class engages in whole-class discussions about various aspects of the problem. Later in the video, a college professor meets with the four members of one student group to present several transfer tasks and probe their reasoning about the tasks. Finally, the teacher reflects on the benefits of the activity.

Designing Experiments in Seventh Grade

A seventh-grade teacher has students work in small groups to study how three factors (length, weight, and angle/height) affect a pendulum's oscillation rate. The first part of the video focuses on the experiments and discussions of a particular group of four students. After the group work, the teacher conducts a whole-class lesson on the importance of separating and controlling variables in scientific experimentation. Later, a college professor gives four students a transfer task that also involves the separation and control of variables. Finally, the teacher describes what students presumably had learned prior to the activity and reflects on the lesson's effectiveness.

Windows on Classrooms: Video Case Studies
This videotape presents four classroom lessons in action, as follows:

#1: The Properties of Air in First-Grade Science: A first-grade teacher conducts a lesson on the properties of air. She introduces the lesson and piques students' interest by asking, "Is air real?" She conducts several demonstrations to illustrate the points that air occupies space and that it puts pressure on other objects. Students then gather in small groups to perform the same experiments themselves. Finally, the teacher reconvenes the children to summarize the things the class has discovered. (14 minutes)

#2: Climate, Geography, and Economics in Junior High Social Studies: A ninth-grade geography teacher conducts a lesson in which students consider data related to the climate, geography, and economics of four different regions of the country. By alternating between (1) asking students to discuss higher-level questions in pairs and (2) conducting whole-class discussions that allow the student pairs to share their conclusions with their classmates, she ensures that most or all of her students are actively thinking about the material that they are studying. (16 minutes)

#3: Graphing in Second-Grade Math: Students in a second-grade classroom gather and graph numerical data within the context of several authentic activities, answering questions related to: (a) the class's favorite jellybean flavor, (b) the month of the year in which each child's birthday falls, (c) the most common mode of transportation that the members of the class use to get to school, (d) the price of a large pepperoni pizza at various pizza places around town, and (e) the times that different children take to run a course. The teacher also has the students translate some of the questions she poses into a traditional addition or subtraction format. (14 minutes)

#4: *The Scarlet Letter* in High School English: A high school English class discusses Nathaniel Hawthorne's *The Scarlet Letter*, with a particular focus on two characters, Reverend Arthur Dimmesdale and Hester Prynne. The teacher uses a variety of strategies, including whole-class discussions, small-group discussions, and brief writing assignments in student "logs," to encourage multiple interpretations of the novel and to make it come alive for her students. (16 minutes)

Educational Psychology Video Package: Video I
This videotape consists of six segments, as follows:

#1: Piaget and Kohlberg: The first part of this segment shows students giving preoperational, concrete operational, and formal operational responses to several conservation tasks. The second part describes and illustrates Kohlberg's preconventional and conventional stages of moral development within the context of a cheating dilemma. (15 minutes)

#2: Cognitive Strategies: This segment shows three teachers promoting more effective learning and study strategies. A kindergarten teacher asks questions that encourage students to relate a story to their personal experiences and to make predictions about what will happen next in the story. A seventh-grade reading teacher engages her students in a reciprocal teaching dialogue. A college professor describes a group of study strategies collectively known as SQ4R—survey, question, read, reflect, recite, and review. (21 minutes)

#3: Cooperative Learning: This segment discusses the key elements of cooperative learning, especially within the context of Robert Slavin's STAD (Student Teams Achievement Divisions) approach. It identifies and illustrates critical components of effective cooperative learning activities. (12 minutes)

#4: Classroom Management: This segment shows a second-grade teacher discussing classroom rules during the first and second weeks of school. It visits the same classroom two months later, showing how the teacher continues to keep students on task as she applies her rules in a variety of classroom activities (e.g., reading, math, cursive writing). (30 minutes)

#5: Lecture-Recitation Model: This segment presents excerpts of a fifth-grade teacher's lesson on the Civil War. It includes expository instruction, teacher questioning, and an assignment involving a written essay. It illustrates many excellent strategies for promoting higher-level thinking skills. (15 minutes)

#6: Classrooms in Action: This segment shows three high school teachers in action—the first teaching about résumés and job applications, the second discussing aspects of the Vietnam War, and the third teaching Charles' Law regarding the relationship of the temperature and volume of a gas. Viewers are asked to consider whether each teacher is effective and whether students are attentive and on task. (39 minutes)

Educational Psychology Video Package: Video II

This videotape consists of five segments, as follows:

#1: Teaching for Learner Diversity: This segment includes three episodes within a single first-grade classroom—a science lesson, student book reports, and whole language instruction. The teacher demonstrates strategies for building on students' previous knowledge and experiences, and for teaching school subject matter in an interdisciplinary fashion. (25 minutes)

#2: Reflecting on the Multiple Roles of Teachers: In this segment, a teacher is depicted in various teaching roles: assessing and monitoring student learning, planning, physically arranging the classroom, managing student behavior, teaching, communicating with a parent, and collaborating with a colleague. The teacher reflects on her various roles as a teacher and on the relative importance of cognitive, affective, and social objectives. (21 minutes)

#3: Essential Teaching Skills: This segment depicts a junior high school science teacher giving a lesson on worms and parasites and how they affect other animals. The video instructs students to evaluate the lesson on the basis of such criteria as organization, focus, feedback, monitoring, and questioning. (17 minutes)

#4: Involving Students Through Group Work: This segment illustrates three possible uses of cooperative learning: (1) to facilitate students' review of classroom material, (2) to teach study skills, and (3) to teach complex cognitive processes. (16 minutes)

#5: Teaching Whole Language: A first grade teacher reads a book about a peanut butter and jelly sandwich and then has students engage in three elaborative follow-up activities: (1) drawing a picture of their favorite food and writing a sentence about the picture, (2) putting several sentences about the story in the correct order, and (3) writing a story about their favorite sandwich. (11 minutes)

Observing Children and Adolescents in Classroom Settings

The segments on this video are designed to enhance students' observational skills. Each video segment is accompanied by one or more *Observation Record* forms that ask students to look for specific behaviors and characteristics as they watch children, adolescents, and teachers in action. (These forms are located in the "Handouts" section near the end of this manual.) The fourteen segments are as follows:

#1: Portfolio: This segment shows a girl named Keenan reviewing samples of her work with her second-grade teacher. The two examine Keenan's progress in spelling, grammar, and reading over the past two years. (5 minutes)

#2: Painting Class: In this segment, an elementary school student named Paula is being interviewed while she is painting a landscape scene. She and her classmates have been learning about Monet and other impressionists and the techniques that these artists used. (2 minutes)

#3: Piaget Tasks: This segment is a duplicate of the first portion of the "Piaget and Kohlberg" segment in Video 1 of Merrill's *Educational Psychology Video Package*. ($6^1/_2$ minutes)

#4: Designing Experiments: This segment presents excerpts from the Merrill video *Insights into Learning: Designing Experiments in Seventh Grade*, in which a group of four students test the possible effects of weight, length, and angle (height of drop) on a pendulum's swing. ($7^1/_2$ minutes)

#5: Pendulum Presentation: This segment shows five elementary school students presenting a report on the results of their experiments with a pendulum. The students have clearly been unable to separate and control variables, and they erroneously conclude that weight affects a pendulum's swing. ($4^1/_2$ minutes)

#6: Birdwatching: This segment shows several young children visiting a nature center, where a naturalist helps them observe and learn about birds in their local area. ($1^1/_2$ minutes)

#7: Balance Scales: This segment presents excerpts from the Merrill video *Using Balance Beams in Fourth Grade*. It shows several fourth graders discussing various solutions to balance scale problems with educational psychologist Dr. Paul Eggen. (12 minutes)

#8: Yeast Discussion: In this segment, a middle school science class is looking at yeast under a microscope and discussing whether yeast is a form of life. ($1^1/_2$ minutes)

#9: Author's Chair: This segment shows several students in a second-grade class reading the stories they have written about field day events earlier in the week. Other students in the class critique each story. (9 minutes)

#10: *The Scarlet Letter*: This segment presents excerpts from the Merrill video *The Scarlet Letter in High School English* (one of the case studies on the *Windows on Classrooms* videotape). The excerpts focus on students' understandings of the motives, beliefs, and actions of the two main characters in the novel. ($5^1/_2$ minutes)

#11: Kohlberg's Stages: This segment is a duplicate of the second portion of the "Piaget and Kohlberg" segment in Video 1 of Merrill's *Educational Psychology Video Package*. ($2^1/_2$ minutes)

#12: Blaine: This segment shows an interview with Blaine, a tenth grader who has a physical disability and a learning disability. Blaine discusses his career objectives, the cause and effects of his disabilities, and his friendships at school. ($5^1/_2$ minutes)

#13: David: This segment shows an interview with David, a high school senior who discusses his friendships with students who have disabilities, and especially his friendship with Blaine. (10 minutes)

#14: Castle Discussion: This segment shows two middle school boys describing recent lessons and activities in a unit on medieval Europe. One of the boys is an Asian immigrant who is learning English as a second language. The two boys describe social interactions that have been an outgrowth of the unit. (5 minutes)

A PRIVATE UNIVERSE:
MISCONCEPTIONS THAT BLOCK LEARNING

Brief Description: The video opens on a graduation ceremony at Harvard University. New graduates are asked simple questions related to astronomy—in some cases, to explain why we have different seasons in the year, and in other cases, to explain why the moon has different phases. Most of the students and faculty members interviewed offer incorrect explanations for these phenomena. The scene then shifts to a nearby high school, where ninth graders (who have as yet had little or no instruction related to the two phenomena in question) offer answers similar to those of Harvard students. The responses and reasoning of one especially capable ninth grader are depicted both before and after instruction. Although the student shows improved understanding after instruction, questions that probe into her reasoning reveal that she still holds on to some of her prior misconceptions.

Relevant Chapter: Chapter 7

Duration: The video lasts approximately 18 minutes.

Using the Video with Chapter 7

You can use the video to illustrate the widespread existence of misconceptions related to common scientific phenomena—misconceptions held not only by high school students, but often by college graduates as well. In many cases, such misconceptions persist despite instruction intended to correct them.

Before you begin: Remind your class that although it is usually beneficial to relate new information to what one already knows, there is an exception to the rule: Learning is *hindered* when one relates new information to previously acquired misconceptions about the world. Tell the class that the video illustrates just how resilient misconceptions about scientific phenomena can be, even after instruction regarding more scientifically accurate interpretations of those phenomena.

You should assume that many of your students may *not* know the scientifically accepted explanations for either the four seasons or the phases of the moon. Therefore, before showing the video, you may wish to ask this question:

- <u>What are the scientifically accepted explanations of the seasons of the year and the phases of the moon?</u>
  Seasons of the year: The seasons are the result of the changing angle at which the sun's rays hit different parts of the earth's surface. The more closely that the rays hit the surface in a "direct" fashion (i.e., at a 90-degree angle), the warmer the temperature becomes. The more that the rays hit the surface "indirectly" (i.e., at a slant), the cooler the temperature becomes. Because the earth's axis is tilted relative to the earth's orbit around the sun, the northern hemisphere receives more direct rays during one half of the year, whereas the southern hemisphere receives more direct rays during the other half of the year.
  Phases of the moon: Except in the event of a lunar eclipse (when the earth comes directly between the sun and the moon), one half of the moon is always illuminated by

the sun. However, the amount of the illuminated moon surface that people on earth can see changes as the moon revolves around the earth (with one complete revolution occurring once approximately every $27\frac{1}{2}$ days). A full moon occurs when the earth is almost between the sun and the moon (although not exactly between them, as this condition would produce a lunar eclipse). A new moon occurs when the moon is almost between the sun and the earth (although not exactly between them, as this condition would produce a solar eclipse). A half moon occurs when the moon is "beside" the earth relative to how the earth lines up with the sun.

After the video: You may wish to ask questions such as these:

- <u>What misconceptions are common regarding to the seasons of the year and the phases of the moon?</u>

   The seasons are often explained in terms of the earth's changing distance from the sun during the year. This explanation makes no sense, however, when you consider that when it is summer in the northern hemisphere, it is *winter* in the southern hemisphere.

   The phases of the moon are often explained in terms of a shadow that the earth casts on the moon. Such an explanation is accurate with regard to a partial or full lunar eclipse, but it is inaccurate with regard to the phases of the moon. In the video, we also see a high school student attribute the phases of the moon to the fact that clouds are blocking part of it from view.

- <u>What evidence do we see that Heather has constructed her own unique understanding of the four seasons?</u>

   As she explains the reasons for the seasons, she initially describes the earth's orbit around the sun as having a "curlicue" elliptical shape with loops on either end. Furthermore, although she correctly understands that the sun's rays are direct in the summer and indirect in the winter, she believes that "indirect" rays are those that bounce off another object before reaching the earth. Heather has presumably never been taught such misconceptions; instead, she has constructed them by combining various pieces of information she has received using her own assumptions about how those pieces should logically fit together.

- <u>From where might the students' misconceptions have originated?</u>
  - Many misconceptions are likely to be the result of constructive processes during either storage or retrieval.
  - In some cases, students may actually be given misinformation by others (parents, teachers, peers, etc.).
  - The video speculates that the common belief that the seasons are caused by the varying distance of the earth from the sun, rather than from the changing tilt of the earth's axis relative to the sun, results from the "side view" perspective of the orbit frequently depicted in science textbooks.
  - The term *indirect*, which is often used in instruction about the seasons, may have contributed to the confusion. In many contexts (e.g., taking an "indirect route" to go somewhere), *indirect* refers to a path that in some way deviates from a straight line.
  - Heather speculates that her own misconception about the "curlicue" nature of the earth's orbit emerged when she confused the orbit with another diagram she had seen in her earth science textbook.

- <u>Two of the Harvard students interviewed describe themselves as having considerable science background. Why might these students continue to hold misconceptions about basic scientific phenomena despite such background?</u>
  - They have reinterpreted the scientific explanations they've been taught so as to be consistent with current beliefs; in other words, they have learned those explanations "meaningfully" yet incorrectly.

- They have learned the scientific explanations in a rote fashion and so have not related them to existing beliefs. Hence, although both the misconceptions and the correct explanations are stored in memory, the students do not notice the inconsistency between the two. This is particularly likely to be so if students' misconceptions have not been specifically addressed (so not retrieved from long-term memory) during instruction.

DOUBLE-COLUMN ADDITION:
A TEACHER USES PIAGET'S THEORY

Brief Description: This video, based on Dr. Constance Kamii's applications of Piaget's theory, shows children in a second-grade class developing strategies for adding and subtracting two-digit numbers. The teacher does not directly teach such strategies; instead, she helps the children construct their own strategies by presenting problems, asking for possible solutions, and encouraging class discussion of different approaches. The students develop a variety of creative strategies for adding and subtracting two-digit numbers, many of which reflect a true conceptual understanding of place value in two-digit numbers.

Relevant Chapters: Chapters 2 and 7 and "Learning in the Content Areas"

Duration: The video lasts approximately 20 minutes.

Accompanying Materials: Three transparency masters for the video (Transparencies MG.3, MG.4, and MG.5) are located in the "Transparency Masters" section at the end of this manual.

Using the Video with Chapter 2, Chapter 7, or "Learning in the Content Areas"

You can use the video to illustrate the process of knowledge construction within the context of Piaget's theory (Chapter 2), knowledge construction in general (Chapter 7), or mathematics instruction ("Learning in the Content Areas").

Before you begin: Describe the video as an example of how a second-grade teacher helps students develop strategies for adding and subtracting two-digit numbers not by teaching those strategies directly, but instead by encouraging students to develop their *own* strategies. Explain that the narrator is Dr. Constance Kamii, a woman who has written extensively about Piaget's theory and its classroom applications. Ask your students to be on the lookout for specific techniques that the teacher uses to encourage the children to construct and reflect on different approaches to solving arithmetic problems.

After the video: You may wish to ask such questions as these:

- <u>What strategies does the teacher use to encourage her students to develop their own strategies for adding and subtracting two-digit numbers?</u>
  - She specifically does *not* teach the children a particular strategy for solving the problems she writes on the board. For example, after giving the class its first two-digit addition problem ("13 + 13"), she asks, "What's the best way to get this answer?"
  - She emphasizes how important it is that students *think* about what they are doing. For example, after she writes the problem "9 + 6" on the board, she says, "Raise your hand if you have a way to get this answer by thinking about it."
  - She waits for several seconds, usually until most of the children have raised their hands to indicate that they have arrived at a solution. (If students have previously read Chapter 6, you can refer to the concept of *wait time* here.)

- She encourages students to explain and defend the solutions they arrive at.
- She solicits a variety of *different* approaches to solving each problem.

- What kinds of strategies do the students develop?

  The three transparency masters provided for this video illustrate some of their strategies.

- As two-digit addition and subtraction skills are typically taught, the process begins by adding the digits in the "ones" column. Yet many of the children's invented strategies begin in the "tens" column instead. Why might this be the case?

  One possibility is that the numbers in the tens column are, in a sense, more "critical" to the problem: They enable the children to arrive at a ballpark figure relatively quickly, then make minor adjustments based on the digits in the ones column. Another possible explanation is that the children naturally move from left to right, just as they do when they read.

- How does the teacher encourage her students to reflect on inadequate strategies?

  She encourages multiple answers to the same question or problem, and she has her students respond to their classmates' ideas with either "Agree!" or "Disagree!"

- What are the advantages of asking students to explain and defend their strategies to the entire class?

  - By verbalizing their ideas, students must first clarify those ideas for themselves. In the words of Dr. Kamii, "When students try to give an argument to convince somebody else, this thinking itself helps them learn math."
  - A situation is created in which students encounter perspectives different from their own. As Dr. Kamii says, "If they become convinced that another idea is better, they will change their minds. This is why a teacher refrains from saying that an answer is correct or incorrect, and instead encourages children to agree or disagree with each other."
  - There may be a motivational advantage as well. The children frequently request the opportunity to defend their choices, calling out, "I can prove it!"

- Dr. Kamii points out that the children never had worksheets or other drill work when they studied arithmetic in first grade. What advantages and disadvantages might such drill work have?

  On the one hand, such drills could improve automaticity of basic arithmetic facts. On the other hand, drills do not promote a meaningful understanding of numbers or arithmetic operations; they may even encourage a *rote* approach to mathematics.

If you are using the video in conjunction with Chapter 7 or "Learning in the Content Areas," you may also want to ask:

- What evidence do you see that the children have a conceptual understanding of place value?

  They manipulate numbers in a variety of creative ways to solve arithmetic problems, resulting in strategies that they have never been taught. At one point, the teacher specifically asks if anyone has misinterpreted the "1s" in "13 + 13," but the children affirm that the 1s are actually equal to 10s.

Insights into Learning

USING BALANCE BEAMS IN FOURTH GRADE

Brief Description: A fourth-grade teacher has students work in small groups to solve problems involving weights on a balance scale. The first part of the video looks at how a group of four students (Molly, Drexel, Susie, and Tad) analyzes problems and sometimes disagrees about correct solutions. Later, the teacher conducts a whole-class discussion in which she has various students present and defend some of their problem solutions. Following the class discussion, Dr. Paul Eggen meets with Molly, Drexel, Susie, and Tad to present additional problems and probe their reasoning. Finally, Dr. Eggen asks the teacher to reflect on the lesson.

Relevant Chapters: Chapter 8 and "Learning in the Content Areas"

Duration: The video lasts approximately 57 minutes. The running time is displayed continuously throughout the video.

Accompanying Materials: A transparency master for this video (Transparency MG.6) is located in the "Transparency Masters" section at the end of this manual.

Using the Video with Chapter 8 or "Learning in the Content Areas"

You can use the video to demonstrate the nature of children's reasoning during a mathematical problem solving task. If you use the entire video and engage your students in extensive discussion, you should allocate at least 90 minutes of class time. As an alternative, you may want to use only two parts of the video; if so, stop the video at 14:27 (before the whole-class discussion), begin it again at 23:00 (at the start of the follow-up interview with the four students), and then stop it at 40:00.

Before you begin: Describe the general principle that governs how various weights on opposite sides of a balance scale can be combined to make the scale balance:

> Each weight placed on the balance should be multiplied by the distance it is placed from the fulcrum. The total of weight-distance products on one side should equal the total of weight-distance products on the other.

Use the transparency to describe the first problem the children are given:

> The left side of the balance beam has 4 weights at a distance of 8. The right side has 1 weight at a distance of 2. Where on the right side might you place one or more additional weights to make the beam balance?

Ask the students to identify at least two solutions to the problem (e.g., 3 weights at a distance of 10, or 5 weights at a distance of 6) and explain why these solutions should make the scale balance (i.e., the total of the weight-distance products on each side should equal 32).

During the video: Following are some suggestions for places to stop the video (indicated by running times displayed on the screen) and ask questions:

Part 1: Small-group work (beginning of the video to 14:27)

02:30   Notice that the teacher has *not* presented a specific principle or procedure that the students should use to solve the problem. What might be her reasoning here?
> The teacher wants her students to develop strategies for working together and for solving problems. (At the beginning of the video, the narrator states that two objectives for the lesson are to "work collaboratively" and to "improve problem-solving skills"; unfortunately, these vague objectives don't communicate very much.) In addition, the teacher may also want to find out what beliefs students may currently have about a balance scale. (If you are using the video in conjunction with "Learning in the Content Areas," you might talk about student's beliefs in terms of *personal theories* related to science.)

04:55   Molly presents a correct solution. Does she also give a correct rationale?
> Yes. She multiplies the number of weights at a given location by the distance they are from the fulcrum; she also adds the weight-distance products.

05:30   Why might Susie be trying to copy Molly's answer?
> Although we can only speculate, one possibility is that Susie is unsure about how to proceed with the problem and so looks to someone else for guidance.

11:00   The teacher has just explained the principle of the balance scale. Is her explanation clear?
> No, it is vague and difficult to follow.

11:55   Susie says, "It kinda sunk in." Does she now understand the balance scale principle?
> She presents no real evidence that she does. As will become evident later on, she does *not* yet understand the principle.

14:27   At this point, the teacher begins a whole-class discussion of the problem. *If you are using the Short Version, fast-forward to Part 3 at 23:00.*

Part 2: Whole-class discussion (14:27 to 23:00)

17:02   The teacher asks, "Does anybody have another explanation for why that would work?" What is she doing here?
> A student has given a correct solution but an *in*correct rationale; she has argued that for the scale to balance, there should be an equal number of tiles on each side. The teacher is looking for a rationale that includes the distances from the fulcrum as well as the number of weights.

22:40   Has Susie mastered the balance scale principle?
> Not yet.

Part 3: Follow-up interview with Molly, Susie, Drexel, and Tad (23:00 to 40:00)

24:33 <u>Dr. Eggen asks the students to come up with as different solutions as they can. What might be the purpose of identifying multiple solutions?</u>

He can better assess students' understanding of the principle if they identify multiple solutions. He may also want to communicate the idea that there is not always just one "right" answer to mathematical problems.

26:55 <u>Tad says that to balance 4 weights at a distance of 3 on one side, you can put 4 weights at a distance of 3 on the other. Has he mastered the balance scale principle?</u>

Not necessarily. If he believed that *number* of weights alone or *distance* of weights alone affects the balance, he might offer this solution. We see no evidence that he understands that *number times distance* is important.

29:30 <u>Susie has suggested that Dr. Eggen add 2 weights (at 5) to the left side and then place 5 weights (2 at 1, 1 at 2, and 2 at 9) to the second side. Does she understand the principle?</u>

No. She is still considering only the number of weights on each side.

31:00 <u>Do Molly and Drexel understand the principle? Does Tad understand the principle?</u>

It appears that Molly and Drexel do, because they consistently identify correct solutions. They have difficulty verbalizing the principle in a precise manner, however. Tad simply says, "Same as them, I guess." There is no evidence that he actually understands.

32:00 <u>Is Susie making any progress?</u>

It appears that she is. When she says that "The ends kind of bring it down more," she shows a glimmer of understanding that distance has an effect.

32:13 <u>Is Tad making any progress?</u>

Not really. He is making a guess based simply on how the scale initially appeared after one weight was placed at 9.

37:26 <u>Does Tad understand the principle?</u>

At this point, it appears that he does, as he presents a correct rationale.

40:00 <u>Does Susie understand the principle?</u>

Yes. *If you are using the Short Version, this is a good place to stop the tape.*

Part 4: Teacher reflections on the activity (40:00 to end)

45:43 (if students have previously read Chapter 2) <u>Dr. Eggen says that Susie is *centering*—a Piagetian notion referring to the tendency of preoperational children to focus on one dimension of an object or situation to the exclusion of others. From Piaget's perspective, Susie, as a fourth grader, is most likely to be in the concrete operational stage rather than in the preoperational stage. How else might we explain Susie's reasoning?</u>

As indicated in Chapter 2, students reason at more advanced levels when they have more knowledge about a topic. Susie may simply be suffering from a lack of knowledge about balance scales.

46:12   <u>The teacher points out that Tad knows he is probably wrong. In contrast, Susie consistently shows confidence in her responses. Other things being equal, which student would be in a better position to learn the principle?</u>
Tad, who has no misconceptions to interfere with new learning.

47:05   <u>The teacher thinks that she should give her students more practice in "mental math." What purpose(s) might such practice serve?</u>
The teacher herself does not provide a good explanation; we might wonder if she's adopting a "formal discipline" philosophy of transfer. In any case, we must remember that mental math involves working memory, and practice can certainly not "enlarge" students' working memory capacity. However, it might enhance students' automaticity for number facts, or it might encourage students to develop strategies for using their existing working memory capacity more effectively.

After the video: You may wish to ask such questions as these:

- <u>Does the teacher ever provide a good explanation of the balance scale principle?</u>
  Not really. Students who are struggling to understand the principle would probably not benefit from her imprecise explanations.

- <u>Have Molly, Drexel, Susie, and Tad all mastered the principle?</u>
  Molly and Drexel appear to have mastered the principle early in the small-group problem-solving session. Susie and Tad offer correct rationales near the end of the interview session. However, it would probably be wise to re-assess their understanding again at a later time.

Insights into Learning

FINDING AREA IN ELEMENTARY MATH

Brief Description: Within the context of an authentic activity (determining how much carpet will be needed to cover a portion of the classroom floor), a fifth-grade teacher has her students work in small groups to find the area of an irregular shape. She displays a transparency that depicts five steps in problem solving and uses these steps to guide the activity. Periodically the class engages in whole-class discussions about various aspects of the problem. Later in the video, Dr. Donald Kauchak meets with the four members of one student group to present several transfer tasks and probe their reasoning about the tasks. Finally, the teacher offers her reflections on the benefits of the authentic activity.

Relevant Chapters: Chapters 8 and 13 and "Learning in the Content Areas"

Duration: The video lasts approximately 56 minutes. The running time is displayed continuously throughout the video.

Accompanying Materials: A transparency master for this video (Transparency MG.7) is located in the "Transparency Masters" section at the end of this manual.

Using the Video with Chapter 8, Chapter 13, or "Learning in the Content Areas"

You can use the video to demonstrate an authentic activity in mathematics that incorporates both small-group and whole-class discussions. If you use the entire video and engage your students in extensive discussion, you should allocate about 85 minutes of class time. As an alternative, you may want to use only the first portion of the video; reasonable ending points are at 20:38 and at 32.10.

Before you begin: Introduce the video by saying that a fifth-grade teacher presents an authentic activity involving mathematics:

> Students are to calculate the amount of carpet needed to cover most of their classroom floor. Because some of the floor is covered by furniture or needs to remain as uncovered linoleum, the shape is an irregular one.

Explain that the teacher uses small-group work and whole-class discussions throughout the activity, and point out that she begins the activity by reviewing the concepts *perimeter* and *area*.

During the video: Following are some suggestions for places to stop the video (indicated by the running times displayed on the screen) and ask questions:

Part 1: Small-group work and whole-class discussions (beginning of the video to 24:30)

05:00 What are some possible advantages of such a hands-on activity?
- It may make the concept of area more concrete for students.
- It may promote better transfer of mathematics to real-world tasks.
- It may be more motivating.

(You and your students may identify other benefits as well.)

09:00   The teacher has asked the students to evaluate the success of the activity. What might this strategy accomplish?

It gives students a chance to identify (and perhaps to remediate) the difficulties they are having as they try to work together. It also allows students to consider some of the advantages of collaborating with their classmates on difficult tasks.

10:20   The teacher is using a specific list of "Steps in Problem Solving" to guide students as they address the problem. What benefit might using these steps have? *(You can use the transparency to display the five steps.)*

By having the students take the steps one at a time, she teaches them a general approach to problem solving and encourages them to reflect metacognitively on what they are doing.

Are the five steps an algorithm or a heuristic?

They provide a general heuristic that may help students, but they do not guarantee a correct solution.

13:50   What can students gain by tackling the problem in small groups rather than individually?

- They can scaffold one another's efforts on a difficult task (e.g., in the small group, we see one student remind another of something that the latter has forgotten).
- They can keep one another on task.
- They can model effective strategies for one another.
- By explaining and defending their strategies, they must clarify their strategies in their own minds.

(You and your students may identify other benefits as well.)

20:38   The teacher asks the groups to: "Write down three conclusions that your team decided on about the problem." What purpose(s) might this task serve?

Students must reach some consensus about what their group has accomplished, which may encourage them to identify specifically what they have learned. And, as we see in one boy's comments, the task provides an additional opportunity for students to evaluate their effectiveness working with their classmates.

If you are pressed for time, this is one good place to stop the video.

21:40   What's the teacher doing here?

She's asking students to reflect on their cognitive processes related to the problem. She's also communicating the idea that there are often several correct solutions to a mathematics problem.

Part 2: Follow-up interview with one group of students (24:30 to 46:00)

27:10   Dr. Kauchak asks, "So this is an area problem?" From the perspective of cognitive psychology, what is he trying to do by asking the question?

He's trying to help the students encode the problem appropriately.

28:00   The "We Forgot the Closet" problem is similar to the problem the students tackled earlier in the authentic activity. How successfully are they transferring what they learned in that activity to this problem?

Not very well. They are trying to calculate the perimeter rather than the area.

Explain that in the scenes that follow, Dr. Kauchak provides considerable scaffolding for the students and gradually, through a series of questions, guides them to think more appropriately about the problem.

If you are pressed for time, another good place to stop the video is at 32:10.

42:00 <u>After the students developed competence in computing the areas of irregular shapes involving rectangles and triangles, Dr. Kauchak introduced a problem involving the area of a circle. Was this an appropriate step for him to take?</u>
There are likely to be varying perspectives on this question. Some may argue that students cannot readily transfer what they've learned because calculating the area of a circle involves knowing about *pi* (π). Yet others may argue that some aspects of area (e.g., conceptualizing it as being comprised of many little squares) can transfer to some degree.

43:08 <u>Why does Dr. Kauchak ask, "What do you do when you have a funny figure?"</u>
He is asking the students to identify a procedure they can apply to any irregular shape that's comprised of rectangles and triangles. In doing so, he is encouraging them to develop a general principle that may be more easily transferable than specific formulas and/or develop a conceptual understanding of *why* they use the procedures they do.

Part 3: Teacher reflections on the activity (46:00 to end)

In the last ten minutes of the video, the teacher offers some helpful insights about the value of the activity and the importance of group interaction in problem solving. In the interest of time, I suggest that you simply let this part of the video run without interrupting to ask questions.

Insights into Learning

DESIGNING EXPERIMENTS IN SEVENTH GRADE

Brief Description: A seventh-grade teacher has students work in small groups to study the effects of three factors on a pendulum's oscillation rate: length, weight, and angle/height from which the pendulum is dropped. The first part of the video focuses on the experimentation and discussion of one group of four students; the teacher occasionally visits the group to ask questions and provide guidance. After the activity, the teacher reconvenes the class to discuss each group's conclusions and then uses the activity to discuss the necessity to isolate and control variables. Later, Dr. Paul Eggen gives four students a transfer task (feeding puppies using various dog foods) that involves the separation and control of variables. Finally, the teacher describes what students presumably knew prior to the activity and reflects on the lesson's effectiveness.

Relevant Chapters: Chapter 2 and "Learning in the Content Areas"

Duration: The video lasts 59 minutes. The running time is displayed continuously throughout the video.

Using the Video with Chapter 2 or "Learning in the Content Areas"

You can use the video to illustrate the idea that eleven- and twelve-year-olds often have difficulty separating and controlling variables despite prior instruction and experience with this task. If you use the entire video and engage your students in extensive discussion, you should allocate about 90 minutes of class time. As an alternative, you may want to use only a portion of the video; reasonable ending points are at 19:55, 30:10, and 43:32.

Before you begin: Introduce the video as an illustration of how seventh graders are likely to approach a task that requires the separation and control of variables. In the video, a science teacher has students work in small groups to test three variables that might affect a pendulum's oscillation weight: length, weight, and height (the teacher uses the term *angle*) from which the pendulum is dropped. Earlier in the school year, the students had formal instruction about the importance of separating and controlling variables; they also conducted a structured experiment in which they tested the effects of fertilizer, light source, and temperature on plant growth.

During the video: Following are some suggestions for places to stop the video (indicated by running times displayed on the screen) and ask questions:

Part 1: Small-group work (beginning of the video to 19:55)

04:30   Marina has said, "We found out that the shorter it is and the heavier it is, the faster it goes." What's happening here?
      The group is confounding length and weight.

09:00 Paige has just said, "Compare it to the second test now. It's the same height and same paperclips. It's just the length that's different." What's she doing?
>
> She's separating and controlling variables: She's holding height and weight constant while varying length.

09:24 The teacher says, "You need to come up with a conclusion about length. You need to come up with a conclusion about weight. You need to come up with a conclusion about angle." What is he trying to do?
>
> He's providing a structure (scaffolding) that may lead the students to test one variable at a time. However, he is intentionally *not* giving the students a specific procedure to follow.

11:48 What problem is the teacher pointing out?
>
> When the students add each paperclip to the bottom of the preceding paperclip, they are changing the pendulum's length as well as its weight.

13:30 How much scaffolding do these seventh graders need to separate and control variables successfully?
>
> The teacher must provide quite a bit of scaffolding. Most of his scaffolding takes the form of questions intended to steer the students' thinking in particular directions.

15:00 (if students have read Chapter 9) The students conclude that weight influences the frequency of oscillation despite evidence to the contrary. What does the textbook call this tendency?
>
> Confirmation bias.

17:20 Marina says, "The height was higher, but the weight was lower, so it's the same thing." Is she separating and controlling variables?
>
> No. She mistakenly believes that decreasing one variable compensates for increasing another.

18:20 What are they doing now?
>
> They're agreeing to test each variable separately.

19:37 What are they saying now?
>
> Despite the evidence, they've concluded that all three variables affect oscillation rate.

19:55 From Piaget's perspective, would you expect seventh graders to be able to separate and control variables?
>
> According to Piaget, the ability to separate and control variables appears in the formal operations stage. For the average child, this stage emerges at around 11 or 12 years of age. Many seventh graders would still be making the transition from concrete to formal operational thought and so may not have mastered the ability to separate and control variables.

If you are pressed for time, this is one good place to stop the video.

Part 2: Whole-class discussion (19:55 to 24:55)

20:11 The teacher tells the students that when they use different methods, they may get different results. Do you agree with his statement?

48

Unfortunately, students might interpret his statement to mean that the variables may or may not affect the oscillation rate, depending on what experimental procedures were used. In fact, the effects of the variables should *not* be significantly influenced by the experimental procedures.

Part 3: Follow-up interview with one group of students (24:55 to 40:15)

30:10   Have the students learned to separate and control variables?
> It appears that they have, at least within the context of the pendulum problem. However, we would have to wonder whether they would transfer this ability to other problems.

Here is another good place to stop the video.

30:50   (if students have read Chapter 2) Here the group applies the term *controlled variable* to the length. From Vygotsky's perspective, why is it important to use scientific terminology in such instances?
> Vygotsky proposed that adults promote children's cognitive development, in part, by introducing them to the language their culture uses to interpret events.

32:50   By introducing the Puppy Chow vs. Pedigree problem, what is Dr. Eggen trying to do?
> He is trying to determine whether the students can transfer the process of separating and controlling variables to a new situation

40:15   Have the students transferred the ability to separate and control variables?
> Yes, at least when an adult asks them questions that guide their thinking. We have no way of knowing whether they would separate and control variables spontaneously in an unstructured and unguided situation.

Part 4: Teacher reflections on the activity (40:15 to end)

43:32   Consider what the teacher has just said about what his students knew before the pendulum experiment. What does this tell you?
> Formal instruction on the importance of separating and controlling variables and a single structured experience in which students tested one variable while controlling others did not transfer to an unstructured situation. *(If students have previously read Chapter 8, you may want to discuss this phenomenon as an example of situated cognition.)*

Here is another good place to stop the video.

47:20   (if students have read Chapter 8) The teacher has essentially said that the students should be able to separate and control variables in a new situation. Do you agree?
> It is difficult to predict with certainty. Using basic principles of transfer, we could speculate that the students would be more likely to transfer the ability to another school situation (especially one presented in their science class) but less likely to transfer it to an out-of-school context.
>
> In the remainder of the video, the teacher offers additional insights about the lesson. In the interest of time, I suggest that you simply let this part of the video run without interrupting to ask questions.

THE PROPERTIES OF AIR IN FIRST GRADE SCIENCE

Brief Description: A first-grade teacher conducts a lesson on the properties of air. She introduces the lesson and piques students' interest by asking, "Is air real?" She conducts several demonstrations to illustrate the points that air occupies space and that it puts pressure on other objects:

- She places an empty glass upside down into a bowl full of water, removes the glass from the water, and asks students whether the inside of the glass is wet or dry.
- When her students disagree about the wetness or dryness of the glass's interior, she repeats the procedure with a paper towel stuffed inside the glass. The towel remains dry.
- Placing the glass inside the water once again (without the paper towel this time), she tips it slightly to allow air bubbles to escape.
- She puts water inside the glass, holds an index card firmly on top of it, tips the glass upside down, and lets go of the index card. The card stays on the glass, holding the water in.

Students then gather in small groups to perform the same experiments themselves. Finally, the teacher reconvenes the children to summarize the things the class has discovered.

Relevant Chapters: Chapters 7 and 13 and "Learning in the Content Areas"

Duration: The case lasts approximately 14 minutes.

Location: The segment begins approximately 45 seconds into the video.

Using the Video with Chapter 7 or "Learning in the Content Areas"

You can use the video to illustrate strategies for promoting knowledge construction and conceptual change in science.

Before you begin: Introduce the video as an example of how a first-grade teacher tries to help her students construct an accurate understanding of two important properties of air: that it occupies space, and that it exerts force on other objects. Ask students to be on the lookout for instructional strategies that should promote knowledge construction and conceptual change.

After the video: You may wish to ask such questions as these:

- <u>In what specific ways does the teacher make air "real" for her students?</u>
  - She shows them that air keeps water out of a glass that is placed upside down in a bowl of water (e.g., a paper towel stuffed inside the glass stays dry).
  - She creates air bubbles by slightly tipping the immersed glass.
  - She shows them a situation in which water stays inside an upside-down glass, seemingly defying the law of gravity.
  - She allows them to experiment with the water on their own.
- <u>What specific strategies does the teacher use to help her students construct an understanding of the properties of air?</u>
  - She asks students to retrieve their existing knowledge and beliefs about air (e.g., "Is air real?").

- She asks students to explain their reasoning (e.g., "How do you know air is real?").
- She conducts concrete experiments to demonstrate the properties of air.
- She asks students to make predictions ahead of time about what they think will happen in each experiment, thereby eliciting possible misconceptions and encouraging students to compare their predictions with the actual results observed.
- She gives students an opportunity to conduct the experiments themselves.
- She concludes the lesson by asking students to summarize what they have learned.

- Prior to each experiment, the teacher intentionally does *not* tell the class what will happen. Why?

   By not telling the class ahead of time what will happen in each experiment, she is able to solicit students' misconceptions about air. Furthermore, she creates a situation in which students will encounter discrepancies between the prediction they have made and the actual outcome of the experiment.

- After removing the glass from the water in the first experiment, one student claims that the inside of the glass is wet, and the other claims that it is dry. Rather than saying which student is correct, the teacher responds to the difference of opinions by conducting the experiment again, this time with a paper towel stuffed inside the glass. What are the advantages of approaching the disagreement in this way?

   - She helps students to discover the correct answer for themselves, rather than portraying herself as the "source" of everything that they will learn.
   - She implicitly communicates the belief that it's OK to be wrong—that the best approach is simply to collect further data.

- (if your students have previously studied cognitive development) Most first graders are six or seven years old. Is the lesson developmentally appropriate for this age group?

   Yes. From the perspective of Piaget's theory, first graders are likely to be in either the preoperational or concrete operational stages (or making the transition from one to the other). Accordingly, their reasoning is limited to concrete and observable objects and events. The teacher provides concrete illustrations of the points she is trying to make. Furthermore, she tries to explain what the students are seeing as concretely as possible. For example, instead of using the abstract concept *force* to explain why the index card stays on the glass after the glass is turned upside down, she instead talks about the air "pushing" against the card. The act of pushing is concrete and very familiar to first graders.

- Why might *air* be a difficult concept for young children to understand?

   Air cannot be directly observed. In this respect, it is less concrete than solids and liquids.

Using the Video with Chapter 13

You can use the video to illustrate effective use of questioning and structured discovery activities. At the same time, you can use it to foreshadow some of the classroom management strategies presented in Chapter 14.

Before you begin: Introduce the video as an example of how a first-grade teacher tries to help her students construct an accurate understanding of two important properties of air: that it occupies space, and that it exerts force on other objects. Ask your class to consider the specific strategies that the teacher uses as she (1) asks questions, and (2) conducts a structured discovery learning session. Also ask your class to be on the lookout for classroom management strategies that the teacher uses to prevent behavior problems and keep the lesson running smoothly.

During the video: You may wish to stop the video right after the teacher has asked, "How do you know if something is real?" . . . "Is air real?" . . . "How do you know air is real?" At this point, you can ask your class what kinds of questions the teacher is asking. (She is asking higher-level questions—questions that ask students to go beyond the things that they have previously learned about air.)

After the video: You may wish to ask such questions as these:

- In what ways do the teacher's questions promote students' learning and knowledge construction?
  - The many higher-level questions that she asks encourage students to elaborate on (e.g., draw inferences from) the things that they already know.
  - Some questions elicit students' prior beliefs about air, including possible misconceptions.
  - Some questions ask students to justify a response they have given to a preceding question.
  - Some questions ask students to make predictions about what they think is going to happen; when students make incorrect predictions, they encounter discrepant information that may promote conceptual change.
  - At the end of the lesson, the teacher's questions encourage students to summarize the things they have learned (e.g., "What did we learn about air?").
- What specific strategies does the teacher use to help her students discover the properties of air?
  - She shows them that air keeps water out of a glass that is placed upside-down in a bowl of water (e.g., a paper towel stuffed inside the glass stays dry).
  - She creates air bubbles by slightly tipping the immersed glass.
  - She shows them a situation in which water stays inside an upside-down glass, seemingly defying the law of gravity.
  - She allows them to experiment with the water on their own.
- Prior to each experiment, the teacher intentionally does *not* tell the class what will happen. Why?

  By not telling the class ahead of time what will happen in each experiment, she is able to solicit students' misconceptions about air. Furthermore, she creates a situation in which students will encounter discrepancies between the prediction they have made and the actual outcome of the experiment.
- After removing the glass from the water in the first experiment, one student claims that the inside of the glass is wet, and the other claims that it is dry. Rather than saying which student is correct, the teacher responds to the difference of opinions by conducting the experiment again, this time with a paper towel stuffed inside the glass. What are the advantages of approaching the disagreement in this way?
  - She helps students to discover the correct answer for themselves, rather than portraying herself as the "source" of the things that they should learn.
  - She implicitly communicates the belief that it's okay to be wrong—that the best approach is simply to collect further data.
- (to foreshadow ideas presented in Chapter 14) What classroom management strategies does the teacher use to prevent behavior problems and keep the lesson running smoothly?
  - She establishes rules for behavior before she begins the lesson.
  - She captures and maintains her students' attention by having them sit right in front of her on the floor and immediately asking questions that pique their interest.
  - She keeps the lesson moving at a brisk pace, leaving no "down time" in which students have nothing to do.
  - On two occasions, she cues a particular student (Brandon) about appropriate behavior.

- She passes out colored cards that quickly tell students which tables they should go to for the small-group activity.
- She keeps the group activity short ("You have two minutes"), thereby minimizing the likelihood that students will get bored and off-task.
- At the beginning of the small-group activity, she cues appropriate behavior by saying, "I'm looking for helpers."
- Shortly after reconvening the class to conclude the lesson, she cues appropriate behavior when she says, "Wait a minute, Michelle, not everybody's listening. . . now they are."
- She puts her fingers to her lips and quickly says, "Shhh."
- She asks students to line up for the next lesson (which will be conducted somewhere outside the classroom) and reminds students, "Remember to walk."

Windows on Classrooms: Case #2

CLIMATE, GEOGRAPHY, AND ECONOMICS IN JUNIOR HIGH SOCIAL STUDIES

Brief Description: A ninth-grade geography teacher conducts a lesson in which students consider data about the climate, geography, and economics of four different states—Alaska, California, New York, and Florida. She alternates between (1) having students work in pairs to identify similarities and differences among the states and (2) conducting whole-class discussions that allow the student pairs to share their conclusions with their classmates. Later in the lesson, she asks students to identify cause-effect relationships among climate, geography, and economics from the similarities and differences they have identified. Her instructional strategies ensure that most or all students are actively thinking about the material they are studying.

Relevant Chapters: Chapters 6 and 13 and "Learning in the Content Areas"

Duration: The case lasts approximately 16 minutes.

Location: The segment begins approximately 15 minutes into the video.

Using the Video with Chapter 6, Chapter 13, or "Learning in the Content Areas"

You can use the video to illustrate strategies for helping students organize and elaborate on information through a combination of small-group work and whole-class discussions in a social studies class.

Before you begin: Explain that the video depicts a lesson in which a ninth-grade class studies the interrelationships among climate, geography, and economics in different regions of the United States. Prior to this lesson, the class has met in four groups to describe one of four states (Alaska, California, New York, or Florida) with respect to its climate, geographic features, and principal industries. Each group has then entered the data it has collected onto a large matrix on the chalkboard. In the current lesson, the class makes use of the matrix to draw some conclusions. Students should be on the lookout for strategies that the teacher uses to keep her students actively processing the subject matter at hand.

After the video: You may wish to ask such questions as these:
- How does the matrix on the board help students process the material more effectively?
    It helps them organize a great deal of information in a logical fashion.
- What are possible advantages of having students work in pairs, first to identify similarities and differences among the states, and later to draw conclusions and summarize the lesson?
    - All students must actively think about and discuss the material.
    - Some students may feel more comfortable talking to a single student than speaking in front of the entire class.
    - Students can scaffold each other's efforts in answering what may possibly be challenging tasks for ninth graders.

54

- <u>On at least two occasions, students provide ideas that are not necessarily correct. How does the teacher respond?</u>

  When a student says, "They all have cold weather in December," the teacher says, "Okay, we're going to look at that one." When a student says, "They're all in middle latitudes," the teacher points out that, "But Alaska is up to $66\frac{1}{2}$ degrees." In both cases, the teacher doesn't clearly indicate whether the student's response is correct or incorrect, and in both cases she writes it on the board. The teacher is probably thinking that by accepting all responses, she is encouraging student participation. On the other hand, she does not correct the misconceptions, thereby possibly communicating the idea that the responses are correct.

- <u>Near the end of the lesson, the teacher asks her students to draw inferences about cause-effect relationships among climate, geography, and economics (e.g., "Why do they all have forestry?" "Why does each area have tourism?"). Why doesn't she just do this at the beginning of the lesson?</u>

  It may be difficult for the students to draw inferences about cause-effect relationships simply by looking at the data about the four different states. By asking the students to identify similarities and differences among the states first, she is, in essence, helping them elaborate, one step at a time, on the information that they have gathered.

- <u>At one point, the teacher digresses briefly to describe a dogsled race currently underway in Alaska. Does her digression detract from the lesson?</u>

  It is a brief digression that is somewhat related to the topic at hand (i.e., it relates to Alaska's climate), and the teacher quickly gets her class back on task. Therefore, it does not appreciably detract from the lesson. In fact, it relates the lesson to current events—that is, to other things with which some of the students may be familiar.

- <u>At the end of the lesson, the teacher asks the student pairs to develop a summary and conclusions regarding the effects of climate and geography on the economy of the various regions. What advantages does this strategy have?</u>

  By summarizing and drawing conclusions from what they've learned, students must identify the main ideas of the lesson. A second advantage is that the teacher can check to be sure her instructional objectives have been achieved.

- (if your students have previously studied cognitive development) <u>Is the lesson developmentally appropriate for the students? Why or why not?</u>

  The lesson is exclusively verbal and abstract in nature; there are no concrete, hands-on activities. However, such a lesson probably *is* appropriate for ninth graders. From the perspective of Piaget's theory, most of the students should be in, or at least making the transition to, the formal operations stage and so should be capable of abstract thought.

- <u>On two occasions, the teacher refers to a student as "sweetheart." Is this appropriate? Why or why not?</u>

  It probably is not appropriate, because some students are likely to interpret "sweetheart" as a condescending term. On both occasions, the teacher uses it in addressing African American females. Although we cannot draw firm conclusions about a pattern in the teacher's behavior on the basis of two instances, at the same time we would have to wonder if there *is* a pattern in her behaviors toward different students.

Windows on Classrooms: Case #3

GRAPHING IN SECOND GRADE MATH

Brief Description: Students in a second-grade classroom gather and graph numerical data within the context of several authentic activities. The teacher initiates the first activity by asking, "How can I figure out the class's favorite jellybean?" After sampling seven colors of jellybeans, the children "vote" by designating their favorite color on a bar graph. The teacher then has the children use the graph by asking such questions as "How many people liked green?" and "How many more people liked green than red?" When a question that she poses requires addition or subtraction, she encourages the children to "set up the problem" on paper. Following the jellybean activity are four small-group data collection activities related to (a) the month of the year in which each child's birthday falls, (b) the mode of transportation that each child uses to get to school, (c) the price of a large pepperoni pizza at various pizza places around town, and (d) the times that different children take to run a course.

Relevant Chapters: Chapter 13 and "Learning in the Content Areas"

Duration: The case lasts approximately 14 minutes.

Location: The segment begins approximately 30 minutes into the video.

Using the Video with Chapter 13 or "Learning in the Content Areas"

You can use the video to illustrate authentic mathematical problem-solving activities in elementary mathematics.

Before you begin: Introduce the concept of an *authentic activity*—a classroom activity similar to tasks that students are likely to encounter in the outside world—and explain that the video will depict several authentic activities related to collecting and graphing data in a second-grade classroom. Point out that the children depicted in the video have previously had some instruction in construction and interpretation of graphs. Ask your students to be on the lookout for the strategies that the teacher uses to promote problem-solving and transfer.

After the video: You may wish to ask such questions as these:
- What strategies does the teacher use to promote effective problem-solving and transfer?
  Her strategies include these:
  - She places the skills that she is teaching (data collection, graphing, addition, subtraction) within meaningful and real-world contexts.
  - She conducts an open discussion of problem solutions and problem-solving strategies, thereby encouraging students to clarify their procedures and reasoning in their own minds sufficiently to explain them to others.
  - She asks the children to "set up" some of her questions as problems on paper, thereby translating the questions into the traditional format that they have already learned for solving addition and subtraction problems.
  - She says, "How did you solve the problem—that's the most important thing," implying that the objective of the lesson is to focus on learning problem-solving

strategies rather than simply on getting the correct answer. She communicates the same message when she asks "How did you get that?" after a student offers an answer to a problem.
- Through the small-group activities, she gives the children opportunities to practice the skills they have learned in new and different contexts.

- In what ways are the activities "authentic"?
  Examples of possible responses are:
  - The jellybean activity is related to the planning of an upcoming class party.
  - The "pizza" group calls local merchants to inquire about the prices of their pizzas and then uses a computer to construct a bar graph.
  - The "runners" group actually views and times runners via videodisc.

- (if your students have previously studied cognitive development) Is the lesson developmentally appropriate? Why or why not?
  Yes. The teacher teaches the tasks of data collection, graphing, addition, and subtraction within the context of concrete objects and events, consistent with Piaget's notion that seven- and eight-year olds are in the concrete operations stage of cognitive development.

- One child has difficulty understanding the question, "How many more people liked green than red?" and another child initially interprets this question as an addition problem. Why might such a question be a difficult one for second graders to answer?
  Many children in the early elementary grades have difficulty understanding such "relational" questions (see "Learning in the Content Areas"). We could hypothesize a couple of reasons why this might be the case. From a linguistic perspective, the question is a syntactically more complex one than a question such as "How many people liked green?" Furthermore, from the perspective of cognitive psychology, some children may have difficulty keeping all the "pieces" of the question in working memory at the same time.

- (to foreshadow ideas presented in Chapter 14) What classroom management strategies does the teacher use to keep the children on task and the lesson running smoothly?
  - She keeps the children active and engaged throughout the lesson.
  - She uses topics in which the students are naturally interested.
  - She collects the empty plastic bags—potential sources of distraction for the children.
  - During the jellybean activity, she calls the children to the front of the room one table at a time.
  - At one point, she cues a student by saying, "I can't call on you if you're jumping up."

Windows on Classrooms: Case #4

THE SCARLET LETTER IN HIGH SCHOOL ENGLISH

Brief Description: A high school English class discusses Nathaniel Hawthorne's *The Scarlet Letter*, with a particular focus on two characters, Reverend Arthur Dimmesdale and Hester Prynne. The teacher uses a variety of strategies, including whole-class discussions, small-group discussions, and brief writing assignments in student "logs," to make the novel come alive for students. She rarely imposes her own interpretations of the novel on her students; instead, she encourages multiple interpretations and constructions of meaning regarding Arthur Dimmesdale's and Hester Prynne's behaviors.

Relevant Chapters: Chapters 7 and 13 and "Learning in the Content Areas"

Duration: The case lasts approximately 16 minutes.

Location: The segment begins approximately 45 minutes into the video.

Using the Video with Chapter 7, Chapter 13, or "Learning in the Content Areas"

You can use the video to illustrate how a teacher can effectively promote meaning construction within the context of whole-class discussions, small-group discussions, and short in-class writing assignments.

Before you begin: Explain that the video depicts a high school English class that is studying Nathaniel Hawthorne's *The Scarlet Letter*, a novel set in seventeenth century New England. The lesson focuses on two characters, Reverend Arthur Dimmesdale (a stodgy and pious local preacher) and Hester Prynne (a young woman whose husband is absent), who have been carrying on an illicit love affair. When Hester becomes pregnant and bears a child, Dimmesdale remains silent about the fact that he is the father. Ask your students to be on the lookout for strategies that the teacher uses to help her students construct a meaningful understanding of the novel.

After the video: You may wish to ask such questions as these:
- What strategies does the teacher use to help her students construct a meaningful interpretation of *The Scarlet Letter*?
  - She rarely offers her own interpretations, and then only after students have already presented their own.
  - She asks leading questions that encourage students to interpret what they've read. For example, she asks, "What are the clues in the text [that Dimmesdale is the father of Hester Prynne's baby]?"
  - She says, "In your logs, jot down some of the important characteristics of that description [of Arthur Dimmesdale]. What's the diction that strikes you as being essential to understanding Dimmesdale's character?"
  - She also says, "If you were going to draw a portrait of [Dimmesdale], what would you make sure you had?" and suggests that students may actually want to draw a picture of the character.

- As an additional aid to helping students characterize Arthur Dimmesdale, she asks, "What would you keep in mind if you were directing a film of *The Scarlet Letter*?"
- After the students describe Dimmesdale as, among other things, a "nerd," she draws an analogy to George McFly, an awkward, "nerdy" character in the film *Back to the Future*.
- In a previous class meeting, she has had students find pictures of what Hester Prynne might look like.
- After reading a passage in which Arthur Dimmesdale insists that Hester Prynne publicly identify the father of her child, she breaks the class into "Dimmesdales" and "Hesters" and asks students to write in the "voice" of their assigned character. For example, she instructs the Dimmesdales to "Write in Dimmesdale's voice what's going on in your mind behind these public words. What are the private thoughts?" She then has the students break into groups of two Dimmesdales and two Hesters each to compare what they have written.

- What strategies does the teacher specifically use to encourage multiple interpretations of the novel?
    - The teacher elicits numerous ideas regarding Reverend Dimmesdale's character.
    - The small group meetings of two Dimmesdales and two Hesters, followed by a whole-class discussion of the characters' thoughts and motives, yield multiple interpretations.
    - In general, she encourages a variety of perspectives; at no point does she suggest that there is a single "right" interpretation of the novel.

- What are possible benefits of asking students to write their thoughts on paper during the lesson?
    - All students must respond to a question; accordingly, students stay on task.
    - Students are more likely to clarify their thoughts when they must express those thoughts on paper.
    - The assignment that asks students to write in either Dimmesdale's or Hester's "voice" requires students to put themselves in the shoes of a particular character, thereby possibly gaining a better understanding of that character's thoughts and motives.

- From the textbook author's perspective, in what way is the teaching of classic literature consistent with a constructivist view of learning?
    In Chapter 7, the textbook author argues that teachers can help their students make sense of the world, in part, by showing them how others have done so. Classic literature illustrates how others (i.e., authors) have tried to make sense of the human experience.

- (if your students have previously studied cognitive development) Is the lesson developmentally appropriate for high school students?
    Yes. High school students are capable of the abstract thought that predominates in the lesson. In addition, the novel concerns love, forbidden sex, and pregnancy—issues that are concerns for many adolescents.

Educational Psychology Video Package, Video I: Segment #1

PIAGET AND KOHLBERG

Brief Description: The first part of this segment shows elementary school students responding to Piagetian tasks involving conservation of quantity (using clay balls and a discussion of pizza slices), conservation of liquid (using containers of different shapes), conservation of number (using pennies), and separation and control of variables (discussing the possible effects of different dog foods on how quickly puppies grow). Preoperational, concrete operational, and formal operational reasoning processes are depicted. The second part of the segment describes and illustrates Kohlberg's preconventional and conventional stages of moral development within the context of a cheating dilemma.

Relevant Chapters: Chapters 2 and 3

Duration: The entire segment lasts approximately 15 minutes. The first part, dealing with Piagetian tasks, is 11 minutes. The second part, dealing with moral development, is 4 minutes.

Location: The segment begins approximately $1\frac{1}{2}$ minutes into the video.

Using the Video with Chapter 2

You can use the first part of the segment to illustrate preoperational, concrete operational, and formal operational reasoning on tasks involving either conservation or the separation and control of variables.

Before you begin: Give an overview of Piaget's preoperational, concrete operational, and formal operational stages (for example, you might use the supplementary lectures on these three stages presented in the Instructor's Manual). The video specifically asks students to look for instances of *egocentrism*, *centration*, *ability to reason about transformations*, and *irreversibility*, so you may want to give special attention to these four characteristics. Note that centration is not discussed in the textbook; however, you can find an explanation of this concept in the "Piaget's Preoperational Stage" lecture in the Instructor's Manual.

During the video: You may wish to stop the video at several points to explain what your students are seeing:

- After the two responses to the pizza task: The 6-year-old boy, by focusing on the number of pieces without regard to how big each piece must be, is exhibiting centration. In contrast, the 11-year-old girl realizes that the larger size of each slice compensates for the smaller number of slices (thereby showing decentration).
- After the three responses to the balls-of-clay task: The first child (a 6-year-old girl) contradicts herself when she says that the pancake has more because it's "flattened," thus focusing on the dimension in which the pancake is actually *less* than the ball. In doing so, she exhibits centration. Furthermore, she shows no inclination to roll the pancake back into a ball, thereby demonstrating irreversibility. The other two children (7 and 12 years old) show conservation of quantity when they say that the ball and pancake have the same

amount of clay. For example, the third child shows her ability to reason about transformations when she says they're the same "because they're both balls, but one is just flattened out."

- <u>After the two responses to the liquid-and-beakers task</u>: The 6-year-old girl says that one beaker has more because it's "taller," thereby showing centration. The 11-year-old girl shows ability to reason about transformations when she says, "Before, you had two beakers of water with the exact same amount of water in it, and you just poured it into a wider and bigger beaker." She shows decentration when she says, "It makes it look . . . a smaller amount, but it's wider."

- <u>After the two responses to the pennies task</u>: The 6-year-old boy shows both centration and irreversibility when he says, "It's bigger because you spread them out." The 12-year-old girl shows conservation of number when she recognizes that the spacing of the pennies does not affect their amount.

- <u>After the three responses to the puppy food task</u>: The responses of the two boys (6 and 7 years old) show an inability to separate and control variables. For example, the first boy talks about giving both kinds of dog food to the same dog. His response also shows egocentrism because he does not always explain himself in a way that someone else might understand; for example, he says, "You could get one *other* dog" when he hasn't previously discussed any dogs at all. In contrast, the 11-year-old girl designs an experiment that separates and controls variables: she gives each food to five of the puppies.

After the video: You may wish to ask such questions as these:

- <u>Which tasks may involve abstract reasoning? Which tasks clearly involve only concrete reasoning?</u>
  The pizza task, in which the pizza is described but not actually shown to the children, may involve abstract thinking and so might be difficult even for children in concrete operations. Similarly, the dog food task is presented only verbally, so may be fairly abstract in nature. The other three tasks (clay, liquid, and pennies) involve concrete, observable materials.

- <u>How might the teacher have used follow-up questions to elucidate the children's reasoning further?</u>
  The teacher does not always probe the children's reasoning when she needs to, and so we don't always have a complete picture of what they are thinking. When a child says that one beaker has more liquid than the other because "it's taller," she might point out that the liquid in the second beaker is "wider" and see how the child responds. When a child says that one row of pennies has more because "it's spread out," she might point out that each row has six pennies and ask, "Do you still think mine has more? If so, why?" Young children sometimes misinterpret what is being asked of them in Piagetian tasks.*

Using the Video with Chapter 3

You can use the moral development portion of the segment to illustrate preconventional and conventional moral reasoning about a dilemma concerning cheating on a test.

Before you begin: Explain how Kohlberg used moral dilemmas to reveal the nature of children's moral reasoning.

---

* For example, see Margaret Donaldson's *Children's Minds*, 1978, Norton.

After the video: You may wish to ask questions such as these:

- <u>Why do the first two children's responses show preconventional reasoning?</u>
    Both boys focus on the consequences of cheating ("Because he'll get kicked out," and, "The teacher might find out").

- <u>Why do the last two children's responses show conventional reasoning?</u>
    Both girls describe society's conventions ("Because he would be getting somebody else's grade instead of his grade," and, "He should have been paying attention earlier in the course").

- <u>What else do you notice about both girls' responses?</u>
    Both girls suggest that the boy might resolve his dilemma by explaining his situation to his teacher. In this respect, their responses reflect Carol Gilligan's belief that moral reasoning often involves seeking a compromise that addresses everyone's interests.

- <u>How might an individual respond to the cheating dilemma in a postconventional manner?</u>
    There are numerous possible answers here. For example, one might talk about the importance of trust between two people as a social contract or the importance of honesty as an abstract principle.

Educational Psychology Video Package, Video I: Segment #2

COGNITIVE STRATEGIES

Brief Description: This segment shows three teachers promoting more effective learning and study strategies. In the first episode, a kindergarten teacher reads a short story to her students; she occasionally stops to ask questions that encourage students to relate the story to their own personal experiences and to make predictions about what will happen next. In the second episode, a seventh-grade reading teacher reviews the four strategies used in reciprocal teaching; she and her students then engage in a reciprocal teaching dialogue regarding a passage about General Custer. In the third episode, a college professor describes a group of study strategies collectively known as SQ4R—survey, question, read, reflect, recite, and review.

Relevant Chapters: Chapters 6, 8, and 13

Duration: The entire segment lasts approximately 21 minutes. The first episode (questions about the short story) is 4 minutes. The second episode (reciprocal teaching) is 8 minutes. The third episode (SQ4R) is 9 minutes.

Location: The segment begins approximately $15\frac{1}{2}$ minutes into the video.

Using the Video with Chapter 6

You can use the first episode to illustrate how a kindergarten teacher can use questions to promote both meaningful learning and elaboration.

Before you begin: Review the processes of meaningful learning and elaboration. Explain that elaboration takes a variety of forms—drawing inferences, thinking of examples, making predictions, etc.

During the video: You may occasionally wish to stop the video after the teacher has asked a particular question and ask students what kind of processing (meaningful learning or elaboration) the question is intended to promote.

After the video: You may wish to ask such questions as these:
- Which questions are intended to promote meaningful learning?
  The teacher's questions about word meanings (*squabble, muck, bleat*) are designed to make sure students understand each sentence's meaning. When students don't know what the words mean, she defines them in terms of things with which students are already familiar. She also asks, "If you were riding in the boat, would you want the sheep [bleating] all the time?" thereby encouraging students to relate Mr. Gumby's actions to things they themselves would be likely to do.
- Which questions are intended to promote elaboration?
  When the teacher asks students to predict ("What's going to happen to . . . ?"), she is asking them to go beyond the information itself.

- In what situations do you see children making *inappropriate* connections between the story and the things they already know?

  Some students initially think that "muck" is "mud" or that "bleating" is "bleeding." Here the students are trying to make meaningful connections between the new information and their knowledge base, but their existing vocabulary is insufficient for them to do so correctly.

Using the Video with Chapter 8

You can use the three episodes to illustrate how teachers can promote more effective learning strategies at a variety of age and grade levels.

Before you begin: Review the concept of metacognition, and explain that students don't necessarily develop sophisticated learning strategies on their own. Explain, too, that learning strategies are most effectively taught within the context of specific subject matter.

During the video: You may wish to stop the video after each episode to identify the specific strategies the teacher uses to promote effective cognitive processing.

After the video: You may wish to ask questions such as these:

- To what extent is the kindergarten teacher asking lower-level and higher-level questions? Are her questions appropriate for kindergarten children?

  Some questions (e.g., "What does *bleat* mean?") are lower-level questions if students already know the answers. The same questions are higher-level questions if students are unfamiliar with the answers and have to infer word meanings from the story's context. The prediction questions ("What's going to happen . . . ?") are clearly higher-level questions.

- Reciprocal teaching is often considered to be a way in which teachers can scaffold students' use of sophisticated cognitive processes. What examples of scaffolding did you observe?

  She reviews the four strategies used in reciprocal teaching. She also models these strategies. Scaffolding continues in the teacher's absence as students help one another process the passage.

- Do you think the college professor's lecture about SQ4R was an effective way of helping students develop more effective study strategies? Why or why not?

  It may be helpful to the extent that it raises students' metacognitive awareness of effective strategies. Students are also given a limited amount of time to practice the strategies they have just learned. Ideally, however, the students should have ongoing opportunities to practice a variety of study strategies within the context of many different disciplines, with ample feedback about how effectively they are using those strategies.

Using the Video with Chapter 13

You can use the second episode to illustrate reciprocal teaching.

Before you begin: Review the technique of reciprocal teaching. Explain that it can lead to dramatic improvements in reading comprehension skill; therefore, it may be particularly useful when working with poor readers, including many students who are at risk for academic failure.

During the video: You may wish to stop the video when the teacher turns the teaching responsibility over to a student. At this point, you can ask your class to speculate why doing so is an important part of reciprocal teaching. (*Answer:* Students become more effective information processors when they ask such questions of themselves.)

After the video: You may wish to ask such questions as these:

- Consider the four strategies that reciprocal teaching encompasses: predicting, questioning, clarifying, and summarizing. How does each of these strategies promote effective information processing?

    Predicting requires students to go beyond the information actually presented, so it involves elaboration. Questioning can promote a number of effective storage processes—meaningful learning, elaboration, organization, visual imagery—depending on the specific questions that are asked. Clarifying encourages meaningful learning by helping students connect new information to things they already know and thereby make sense of the information. Summarizing requires students to identify and organize main ideas.

- Which of the four strategies do the students use without the teacher's assistance?

    All four are evident. They summarize ("Does anybody know the main idea?"), question ("Would anybody like to help me construct a test question?"), clarify ("Is there anything that somebody needs to clarify about this paragraph?" "I didn't understand the word in the first paragraph where it said, 'The man's foolishness had inadvertently...'") and predict ("Now we're going to try to predict what the author will say in the next paragraph; without looking at the paragraph, what do you think he will say?").

- Why might reciprocal teaching be more effective than simply asking students to use the four strategies on their own?

    In the group discussion, covert strategies become overt, concrete ones that students can readily observe and model. Furthermore, members of the group can give one another feedback about how effectively each is processing the material.

Educational Psychology Video Package, Video I: Segment #3

COOPERATIVE LEARNING

Brief Description: This segment discusses the key elements of cooperative learning, especially within the context of Robert Slavin's STAD (Student Teams Achievement Divisions) approach. It identifies three key components of effective cooperative learning—group rewards, individual accountability, and equal opportunities for success. Within the context of a seventh-grade math class, the video illustrates the following steps:

1. Planning activities. The teacher constructs group worksheets and answer sheets. She also forms heterogeneous groups of four or five students each.
2. Teaching team etiquette and ground rules. The teacher solicits students' suggestions regarding appropriate ground rules for cooperative groups.
3. Teaching the lesson. The teacher presents information about estimation in an interactive lecture format.
4. Beginning cooperative activities. The teacher illustrates how to foster positive interdependence among group members.
5. Administering the unit test. Each student takes the unit test independently. Some students earn 30 points when they obtain a perfect score. Other students may earn 30 points when they demonstrate considerable improvement over an earlier "baseline" score; less improvement yields fewer points.
6. Computing team points. The teacher bases group points on the average number of points that individual group members have earned. An average score of 25 merits a "gold medal," whereas an average of 20 merits a "silver medal" and an average of 15 merits a "bronze medal."
7. Recognizing team accomplishments. A teacher awards certificates of accomplishment to the members of various groups. Groups also get special privileges if they earn medals; for example, gold medal winners get 20 minutes of free time for their achievement.

Relevant Chapter: Chapter 13

Duration: The segment lasts approximately 12 minutes.

Location: The segment begins approximately 38 minutes into the video.

Using the Video with Chapter 13

You can use the segment to illustrate cooperative learning in action and to highlight key ingredients that maximize its success.

Before you begin: Discuss the advantages of cooperative learning (e.g., it facilitates academic achievement, promotes the development of prosocial behavior, and encourages friendships both across ethnic groups and between disabled and nondisabled students).

After the video: You may wish to ask such questions as these:

- <u>Why is individual accountability important? Why are group rewards also important?</u>
  When there is individual accountability for learning, students cannot slack off and assume that other group members will somehow "cover" for them. Group rewards give students an incentive for helping other group members learn the material.

- <u>The teacher uses improvement as the criterion for success. Some theorists recommend against using improvement as a criterion because it encourages students to hide what they already know by performing especially poorly in the pretest (baseline) situation. In this situation, why will the students probably have little reason to hide what they know initially?</u>
  Students who show little improvement because their pretest scores are high can achieve the highest number of points simply by earning a perfect score on the posttest.

- <u>In what way might cooperative learning groups provide a form of *scaffolding* for students?</u>
  In some cases, one student may be an "expert" who knows a topic or procedure well enough to guide the others through it. In other cases, different group members may each have strengths that contribute to a better final product than any one could accomplish by working alone.

- <u>What does the teacher do to foster positive interdependence among group members? What other things might a teacher do to foster positive interdependence?</u>
  In this situation, each group member receives either a worksheet or an answer sheet, but not both. Other possible ways of promoting interdependence include assigning different roles to different students and giving each group member only a portion of the material that everyone must ultimately learn; the latter approach is frequently called the *jigsaw* technique.

Educational Psychology Video Package, Video I: Segment #4

CLASSROOM MANAGEMENT

Brief Description: This segment identifies and illustrates three essential components of classroom management: defining rules, reviewing them at a later time, and applying both the rules and behavior management techniques during classroom activities. The video follows a second-grade teacher through the first few weeks of school. On the first day of class, she talks with students about the need to have classroom rules and solicits students' ideas as to what some good rules might be. She then presents her own set of rules:
1. Follow directions.
2. Be polite.
3. Obey safety rules.
4. Come to class prepared with supplies and homework.
5. Work quietly and independently using self-control.

A week later, the teacher and her students review the rules and agree that they are working well. Finally, the video visits the same classroom two months later, showing how the teacher continues to keep students on task as she applies the rules in a variety of classroom activities.

Relevant Chapter: Chapter 14

Duration: The segment lasts approximately 30 minutes.

Location: The segment begins approximately $51\frac{1}{2}$ minutes into the video.

Using the Video with Chapter 14

You can use the video to show the importance of developing classroom rules in a somewhat democratic atmosphere. You can also use it to illustrate praise for appropriate behavior and cueing of inappropriate behavior. (Note: I have found that this video promotes a great deal of class discussion: Some students think the teacher is much too controlling, but others think that she uses an appropriate degree of control for children in the primary grades.)

Before you begin: Review important strategies for creating and maintaining a productive learning environment (e.g., developing classroom rules, reinforcing appropriate behavior, etc.). Explain the concepts of *withitness*—knowing what students are doing at all times—and *smoothness*—keeping the classroom focused on a meaningful and logical sequence of instruction, without disruptive breaks in an activity or lesson. (*Smoothness* is not specifically mentioned in the textbook; however, the need for smooth transitions from one activity to another *is* discussed.) Also, describe the use of *cueing* as a nondisruptive means of getting students back on task.

During the video: The video specifically asks viewers to consider these questions:
1. Is the teacher's orientation more positive than negative?
2. Does she demonstrate "smoothness" and "withitness"?
3. Does she use the least disruptive intervention?
4. Are her management techniques effective overall? Why or why not?

You may wish to instruct students to take notes related to the preceding questions and to identify specific strategies that the teacher uses for keeping students on task.

After the video: You may wish to ask questions such as these:

- Is the teacher's orientation more positive than negative?
  She praises appropriate behavior more often than she cues students about inappropriate behavior.

- Does she demonstrate smoothness and withitness?
  She seems to be aware of what her students are doing at all times (withitness) and she keeps her lessons flowing even when she must deal with inappropriate behavior (smoothness).

- Does she use the least disruptive interventions?
  Her interventions rarely interfere with the overall flow and continuity of a lesson.

- Are her management techniques effective overall? Why or why not?
  Her management techniques are consistent with many of the principles of classroom management presented in Chapter 14. Furthermore, most of her students appear to be on task most of the time.

- What strategy does the teacher use to solicit answers from all students simultaneously? Why is this strategy likely to be effective?
  Students respond to yes/no questions with thumbs up or thumbs down. The strategy increases the likelihood that all students will pay attention.

- What specific behaviors does the teacher reinforce? How does she reinforce them?
  The teacher reinforces such behaviors as paying attention, being polite, raising one's hand, working quietly, and following directions. Forms of reinforcement include these:
  - Praise (e.g., "You have your thinking caps on, and I like that," and, "You've done a good job of number 4")
  - Vicarious reinforcement (e.g., "I like the way Jeremy is sitting so quietly," and, "I like what Chris is doing; he's using his number line at the top if he needs to")
  - Calling on students (e.g., "I'll call on Melissa because she's waiting nice and quietly with her hand in the air")
  - Allowing students to work problems at the board (e.g., "You were nice and quiet, David. Would you come up and do the first [problem]?")
  - Premack principle (e.g., "When you've finished and I say you did a nice job, you can take time out and color some of the pictures")

- What strategies does the teacher use to cue students about their off-task behavior?
  At one point, she gently pushes down a student's hand when it is too close to her face. At another point, she puts her finger to her lips to remind students to be quiet. More frequently, though, she uses verbal cues such as these:
  - "I called the tigers. Someone wasn't listening. Sema, the tigers were called."
  - "Back on task, Chris. Remember your English work."
  - "Most of you—I'm waiting on one—have your eyes on me."
  - "Books are closed, Anthony."
  - "Amanda, could you join the rest of the group and be right on task? Jeremy's working hard, and Ginger is, and I know you can do it, too."

- How does the teacher deal with students' incorrect answers? Are her responses likely to encourage or discourage student participation?
  She reminds her students that, "It's all right to be wrong. This is not a test." She also asks them, "What are we going to do if one [of the answers on the board] is wrong? Be polite, keep lips closed." Her remarks clearly indicate tolerance for incorrect answers.

- On what occasion did we see evidence of Piaget's concept of *reversibility* in the math lesson?

    Students: "Eight minus four equals four."
    Teacher: "And if we want to flip it, we'd say . . ."
    Students: ". . . four plus four equals eight."

- Are the teacher's procedures likely to promote moral development, as discussed in Chapter 3? Why or why not?

    The teacher often gives reasons for why certain behaviors are important. Research indicates that such reasons often promote moral development.

- Which of the teacher's strategies would also be useful in a secondary classroom? Which ones would not?

    The three essential components of classroom management (identifying rules, reviewing them, and applying them consistently) have applicability across the entire K–12 spectrum. Some of the more specific things the teacher does (e.g., "Somebody left their thinking cap in [their desk]; they're not with me," and, "Look at these good listeners") are probably more appropriate for the elementary grades than for the secondary grades. Also, the teacher is very controlling in her actions; most secondary students would not need such continual reminders about how to behave nor such frequent praise for appropriate behavior.

Educational Psychology Video Package, Video I: Segment #5

LECTURE-RECITATION MODEL

Brief Description: This segment presents excerpts of a fifth-grade teacher's 50-minute lesson on the Civil War. It includes expository instruction, teacher questioning, and an assignment involving a written essay. It illustrates many excellent strategies for promoting higher-level thinking skills.

Relevant Chapters: Chapters 6 and 13 and "Learning in the Content Areas"

Duration: The segment lasts approximately 15 minutes.

Location: The segment begins approximately one hour and $21^{1}/_{2}$ minutes into the video.

Using the Video with Chapter 6, Chapter 13, or "Learning in the Content Areas"

You can use the segment to illustrate how a teacher combines expository instruction, teacher questions, and an essay assignment to promote effective cognitive processing during a history lesson.

Before you begin: Explain that, from the perspective of cognitive psychology, effective teaching involves helping students process information in meaningful and elaborative ways. Instruct students to be on the lookout for specific strategies the teacher uses to promote meaningful learning and elaboration.

During the video: You might occasionally stop the video as the teacher uses a particular strategy to solicit opinions as to how the strategy might help students process information effectively.

After the video: You may wish to ask such questions as these:
- What specific strategies does the teacher use to facilitate effective cognitive processing? Many strategies are evident, including these:
  - She reminds students that they have previously studied certain new vocabulary words, thereby activating prior knowledge.
  - She describes the objectives of the lesson, enabling students to select aspects that are most important to learn.
  - "I'd like you to have some good questions in your head that we don't answer today." Here she encourages students to consider ways in which they might elaborate on the information and make greater sense of it in the lessons to come.
  - On a map she points out the three major sections of the country prior to the Civil War, thereby helping students to form a visual image of how the country was divided.
  - "Pretend that you are slaves. . . . If you were a slave, what are some things that you might have done to get back at a master?" Here she asks students to relate the experience of slavery to things they themselves might do.

- "If you were a slave and you thought you were going to be beaten, would you scream at your master or would you do something sneaky?" Here she helps students make sense of the slaves' behavior by exploring the motives behind it.
- "This should go in your notes." Here she identifies important information—something she expects students to remember. She also scaffolds note-taking for students who are probably just beginning to develop this learning strategy.
- "Abe Lincoln. . . . What do you think about when you hear that name? Can you describe how you think he might have looked from the pictures you've seen?" Here she activates students' prior knowledge and encourages visual imagery.
- "We had a word in vocabulary the other day that I hope you can remember—that describes the way [Lincoln] looks sometimes and in some pictures. Anybody remember?" She asks students to connect Lincoln's appearance to something they have recently learned—the word *gaunt*.
- "*Civil war* means war within a country—one part of a country against another part of that country. Can you think of a place in the world today where there is civil war or the threat of civil war?" Here she helps students connect an event in American history with current events—in this case, with the dissolution of the Soviet Union.
- "Why else might the North have won?" "What did the South have going for her that she might have won the war?" With these questions, the teacher encourages elaboration of the strengths and weaknesses of both sides of the war and perhaps a more meaningful understanding of why the North eventually won the war.
- "How do you think people in the North felt about people in the South [after the war]? She asks students to relate the motives of the Northerners to the feelings they themselves would be likely to have.
- "[The North] put very many harsh punishments on the South, and that made the coming together of the Union take longer. It would be as if you took one cookie from the cookie jar and were sent to your room for a month and a half." By drawing the analogy, she encourages students to understand the harshness of the punishment at a meaningful level.
- "You look at me so you can get the assignment." She's asking for students' attention.

- The teacher asks students to write an essay about the war that includes certain vocabulary words (*abolitionists, Underground Railroad*, etc.). From the perspective of cognitive psychology, what purposes might this assignment serve?

  The assignment should help students organize aspects of the Civil War, at a minimum by sequencing them chronologically and perhaps also by identifying cause-effect relationships. Furthermore, students are more likely to learn information meaningfully and elaborate on it if they have to describe it to someone else.

- What is the students' homework assignment? What purpose does it serve?

  The assignment asks students to keep the Civil War in mind while writing about what the word *indivisible* means in the Pledge of Allegiance. Students will presumably connect this part of the Pledge of Allegiance to a "lesson" that the country learned from the war.

Educational Psychology Video Package, Video I: Segment #6

CLASSROOMS IN ACTION

Brief Description: This segment shows three high school classrooms in action. In the first episode, an English teacher uses expository instruction and recitation in a discussion about résumés and job applications. In the second episode, a history teacher uses a predominantly lecture format to discuss aspects of the Vietnam War. In the third episode, a chemistry teacher uses a combination of demonstration, discovery, teacher questioning, expository instruction, and seatwork to teach Charles's Law regarding the relationship of the temperature and volume of a gas. Viewers are asked to consider whether each teacher is effective and whether students are attentive and on task.

Relevant Chapters: Chapter 13

Duration: The entire segment lasts approximately 38 minutes. The English class episode is 8 minutes. The history class episode is 13 minutes. The chemistry class episode is 17 minutes.

Location: The segment begins approximately one hour and 37 minutes into the video.

Using the Video with Chapter 13

You can use the video to illustrate three approaches to teaching subject matter at the high school level. It provides an excellent opportunity for students to observe and critique three distinctly different teaching styles. (If you are working under tight time constraints, you may want to show only one or two of the three teaching episodes.)

Before you begin: Explain that there is probably no single teaching strategy that is "best" in all situations, and that virtually any teaching strategy probably has its advantages and disadvantages. Introduce the segments as illustrations of three different approaches to teaching high school subject matter, and ask students to consider the advantages and disadvantages of each as they view the video.

During the video: You may wish to stop the video after each of the three episodes and ask such questions as these:

English class
- What does the teacher do well? What might she do better?
  Responses to these questions will vary. Strengths include many questions that get students involved and activate their prior knowledge about résumés and job interviews; a few are higher-level questions (e.g., "Why do you think you might want to avoid having a relative give you a reference?"). The teacher plans to have students role-play a job interview, which should give them valuable practice applying some of the ideas they are learning. On the other hand, the teacher allows little wait time, especially after students' responses; there are few pauses in the discussion. Furthermore, the presentation is almost entirely auditory, with only a few words on the board as visual aids.

- <u>What do the teacher's instructional objectives appear to be?</u>
  Possible objectives are these:
    - The student will write a resumé that conveys strengths in a convincing manner.
    - The student will identify appropriate references to support a job application.
    - The student will present himself or herself in a conservative, competent, and confident manner.
- <u>How might you teach résumé writing differently than the teacher does?</u>
  Students' opinions on this question will vary. Two possible answers are allowing longer wait time and providing more visual aids.

History class

- <u>What does the teacher do well? What might he do better?</u>
  Answers to this question are likely to vary. Among the teacher's strengths are his enthusiasm and his use of maps. On the other hand, his presentation affords little opportunity for student participation.

- <u>What do the teacher's instructional objectives appear to be?</u>
  The teacher's instructional objectives appear to focus on student knowledge. Possible objectives might include these:
    - The student will demonstrate knowledge of key aspects of the Vietnam War.
    - The student will locate critical places and events of the Vietnam War on a map of Southeast Asia.

- <u>What evidence do you see that the teacher is taking students' prior knowledge into account?</u>
  The teacher reviews yesterday's lesson, which provides a background for today's topic. He also refers to films that students may have seen. And he says things such as, "We've talked about colonies a lot in the past," and "Remember somebody saying that?"

- <u>What kinds of questions does the teacher ask?</u>
  He asks both lower-level questions (e.g., "Remember who [the Secretary of State under Eisenhower] was?") and higher-level questions (e.g., "Can anybody imagine why [the elections] weren't held? What would be a good reason for not holding those elections as they were scheduled?").

- <u>For most of the class session, the teacher is lecturing. What alternative teaching strategies might he use to accomplish his objectives?</u>
  Brainstorming as a group, your students are likely to identify a variety of creative strategies. A few possibilities are showing pictures or slides of the Vietnamese countryside and of important players in the war (e.g., Ho Chi Minh), holding a classroom debate concerning the pros and cons of the war, and illustrating the domino theory with actual dominoes.

Chemistry class

- <u>What does the teacher do well? What might she do better?</u>
  Answers will vary. Among the teacher's strengths are her use of concrete objects to teach an abstract principle, her review of what students have previously learned, and her questioning techniques to encourage students' discovery of Charles's Law. One possible weakness is minimal teacher wait time after students' responses. But perhaps a more serious one is that throughout the entire class session, the teacher calls *only* on boys to answer her questions.

- <u>What do the teacher's instructional objectives appear to be?</u>
  Possible objectives are these:
    - The student will describe Charles's Law.

- The student will apply Charles's Law in problems involving the temperature and volume of a gas.

- <u>The teacher wants students to discover Charles's Law for themselves rather than directly telling them what the law is. What strategies does she use to help them discover Charles's Law?</u>
  At the beginning of the lesson, she places three balloons of equal size in beakers of water of three different temperatures. Later, she asks students to observe how the balloons have changed in size relative to one another. Furthermore, she asks questions to help students recall the things they already know about temperature and volume, lists these things on the chalkboard, and asks students to draw their own inferences about the relationship between temperature and volume.

- <u>In what ways does the teacher scaffold students' efforts?</u>
  The strategy described above—helping students retrieve what they already know and synthesizing that knowledge to derive Charles's Law—is a form of scaffolding. She also looks over students' shoulders as they solve problems on their own, giving them occasional reminders about what they should do (e.g., reminding them to convert temperature to the Kelvin scale).

- <u>At the end of the lesson, the teacher asks students to recap what they have learned. In what ways might the recap facilitate students' retention of the information presented?</u>
  The review and summary help students identify and interrelate the main ideas of the lesson.

- <u>From Piaget's perspective, in what stage of cognitive development must students be in order to understand Charles's Law?</u>
  Proportional reasoning is involved, as is an understanding of such abstract concepts as volume and pressure. Therefore, formal operational thinking is required.

After the video: At the conclusion of the entire segment, you may wish to ask questions such as these:

- <u>How attentive are the students in the three classes? What strategies do the teachers use to capture and maintain students' interest and attention?</u>
  The great majority of students in all three classes appear to be attentive. For example, students in the history and chemistry classes are frequently seen taking notes.
  Strategies for gaining and maintaining students' attention include the following:
  - Asking questions (all three teachers)
  - Writing things on the board (all three teachers)
  - Demonstrating a phenomenon with concrete objects (the chemistry teacher)
  - Relating the subject matter to students' personal needs (the English teacher)
  - Asking students to complete a particular task: to add things to a map (the history teacher) or solve problems (the chemistry teacher)
  - Modeling their own interest in the subject matter (especially evident in the case of the history teacher)
  - Presenting two contradictory ideas—pointing out that the United States, founded on the notion of free elections, supported the fact that no elections were conducted in South Vietnam (the history teacher)

- <u>Imagine that you are a student in all three classes. From which teacher do you think you would learn the most, and why?</u>
  Answers to this question will vary.

Educational Psychology Video Package, Video II: Segment #1

TEACHING FOR LEARNER DIVERSITY

Brief Description: This segment depicts three episodes within a single first-grade classroom. (Its title is somewhat of a misnomer, as all of the students are African American, and there is no evidence that they come from diverse cultural backgrounds; as a group, therefore, they appear to be racially and culturally homogeneous.) The first episode is a science lesson in which the teacher relates plants to students' knowledge of gardening. In the second episode, students give book reports regarding books about animals; here the teacher encourages vocabulary development and relates aspects of the books to things students already know about animals. The third episode illustrates a whole language approach as the class considers the storybook *The Bear's Toothache*. Within this context, the teacher reviews vocabulary, compound words, and root words; she also asks students to identify the characters, setting, problems, and solutions. In addition, three students act out the story itself.

Relevant Chapters: Chapter 6 and "Learning in the Content Areas"

Duration: The segment lasts approximately 25 minutes. The first episode is 10 minutes. The second episode is 8 minutes. The third episode is 7 minutes.

Location: The segment begins approximately 30 seconds into the video.

Using the Video with Chapter 6

The first episode is an excellent example of how a teacher might activate students' prior knowledge as she presents new information.

Before you begin: Explain that students are most likely to connect new information to existing knowledge if both of these are in working memory at the same time. Explain, too, that students do not always recognize relationships between new things and the things they already know, so it is important for teachers to point out the kinds of connections that can be made.

During the video: Stop the video when the teacher stands up to write on the chalkboard. Ask:
- <u>Students on the right side of the room have been more actively involved than students on the left. Why might this be?</u>
  One possible reason is that the teacher has been facing the right side of the room almost exclusively up until now.

You might also stop the video a short time later and ask:
- <u>How much wait time has the teacher been allowing?</u>
  Very little. She responds almost immediately to students' responses. Students typically respond to her questions immediately, so wait time after her questions is also quite short. It appears that the teacher is intentionally maintaining a brisk pace, perhaps as a way of maintaining students' interest and engagement in the discussion.

After the video: You may wish to ask questions such as these:

- What does the teacher do to promote meaningful learning?
    She continues to connect material in the newspaper article to students' experiences with gardening at home, to previous discussions in science, and to a story they have read.

- What does the teacher do to promote elaboration?
    She occasionally asks questions that require students to go beyond the information actually presented. For example, she asks:
    - "What would happen if we left those weeds in there?"
    - "Why should [the water from the garden hose] be soft?"
    - "What do you see in the words [on the chalkboard] that are similar?"

- Is the teacher taking students' limited working memory capacity into account?
    Yes. Although she is moving the class along at a brisk pace, she nevertheless presents each new idea slowly enough that students should be able to process it meaningfully.

- Near the end of the lesson, the teacher incorporates spelling and vocabulary instruction into her science lesson. Is this an effective strategy?
    Probably so. It can help the students see the interdependence of various academic subject areas (in this case, the interdependence of science, spelling, and vocabulary).

Using the Video with "Learning in the Content Areas"

You can use the second and third episodes to illustrate reading activities that might be suitable for first graders.

Before you begin: Introduce the two episodes as illustrations of how a teacher might teach basic reading skills while also promoting an interest in reading.

During the second episode (the book reports): At the end of the first child's book report, ask:

- In his "book report," the boy only shows pictures. Why?
    The book's reading level is well above that of the average first grader. A reasonable guess is that the boy has chosen the book because of his interest in animals but his reading skills are insufficient to allow him to read the book.

- How does the teacher scaffold the student's book report?
    She reminds him to show some of the book's pictures. She also reminds him to hold up the book and make sure everyone can see it. At one point, she identifies a good picture for him to show.

After the second episode: At the end of the second episode, you may wish to ask:

- The teacher often departs temporarily from the book reports to ask students general questions about animals. What purpose might this strategy serve?
    It illustrates the idea that students should think about what they already know about a topic as they read something new about that topic.

During the third episode (whole language instruction): After the teacher says, "Who has the toothache? . . . The bear does," stop the videotape and ask:

- What aspects of language does *The Bear's Toothache* enable the teacher to discuss?
    The teacher reviews the concept of *title*, identifies several new vocabulary words, and talks about compound words and root words. She also reviews key aspects of a short story: characters, setting, problems, and solutions. This process illustrates a *whole*

language approach, in which basic reading skills are taught within the context of authentic reading materials.

After the third episode: At the end of the third episode, you may wish to ask:

- <u>What are some possible advantages of having three students act out the story?</u>
  It might make the story more concrete, and therefore more understandable, for the students. Furthermore, it associates the process of reading with an enjoyable activity, which may have motivational benefits.

Educational Psychology Video Package, Video II: Segment #2

REFLECTING ON THE MULTIPLE ROLES OF TEACHERS

Brief Description: In this segment, a fifth-grade teacher is depicted in several teaching roles:
- Assessment and monitoring of student learning
- Planning
- Classroom management
- Instruction
- Communication with parents
- Collaboration with colleagues

Expository instruction, cooperative learning, and individual seatwork are all illustrated. In an interview, the teacher reflects on her various roles as a teacher and on the relative importance of cognitive, affective, and social objectives.

Relevant Chapter: Chapter 13

Duration: The segment lasts approximately 21 minutes.

Location: The segment begins approximately 27 minutes into the video.

Using the Video with Chapter 13

You can use the video as an introduction to the multidimensional nature of the teaching profession.

Before you begin: Ask students to brainstorm the various roles that teachers serve.

During the video: Stop the video just before Dr. Ross's interview with the teacher begins, and ask the following questions:

- <u>What different instructional methods does the teacher use?</u>
  She uses expository instruction (e.g., as she briefly discusses exploration), cooperative learning, and independent assignments combined with one-on-one assistance.

- <u>Many people describe teaching as a reflective process. About what things must teachers reflect?</u>
  Things identified in the video include:
  - Students' current knowledge and abilities
  - Students' existing learning problems and difficulties
  - Instructional goals
  - Materials appropriate for reaching those goals
  - Effectiveness of the instructional methods being used

- <u>The video emphasizes the importance of teacher planning. What does planning include?</u>
  Things identified in the video include:
  - Planning appropriate lessons
  - Selecting appropriate materials
  - Having materials ready before class begins

- Physically arranging the classroom in a way that facilitates learning and teacher-student interaction

- The teacher talks about effective social skills both before and during the cooperative learning activity. Why is it important that she do this?

  Students will not necessarily have all the social skills necessary for cooperating effectively with one another.

After the video: You may wish to ask questions such as these:

- What is the teacher's number one goal for her classroom?

  "No child has the right to keep another child from learning."

- The teacher claims that her students become increasingly independent learners. What strategies does she use to promote self-regulated learning?

  She uses strategies such as these:
    - Conducting cooperative learning activities in which students are only minimally dependent on their teacher
    - Giving independent seatwork assignments
    - Allowing students to make choices (e.g., among using the restroom, finishing a math assignment, and getting materials ready for the next activity)

  During the interview, the teacher mentions teaching "organizational skills," but it is not clear what she means by this statement.

- What strategies does the teacher use to open the lines of communication between herself and her students' parents?

  At the beginning of the school year, she calls parents and introduces herself. She also makes a concerted effort to show parents that they can trust her.

- The teacher argues that affective objectives may ultimately be more important than cognitive ones. Do you agree with her position? Why or why not?

  Students' opinions on this issue will vary. You may want to list the various perspectives, both pro and con, on a chalkboard or transparency. At the end of the class discussion, you should probably point out that cognition and affect are inextricably intertwined: Achievement of cognitive objectives gives students greater self-confidence, and greater self-confidence keeps students attentive and on task.

Educational Psychology Video Package, Video II: Segment #3

ESSENTIAL TEACHING SKILLS

Brief Description: This segment depicts a junior high school science teacher giving a lesson on worms and parasites and how they affect other animals. The video instructs students to evaluate the lesson on the basis of the following criteria:
- Attitudes
- Organization
- Communication
- Focus
- Feedback
- Monitoring
- Questioning
- Review and closure

Relevant Chapter: Chapter 13

Duration: The segment lasts approximately 17 minutes.

Location: The segment begins approximately 48 minutes into the video.

Accompanying Materials: A handout that accompanies the video (Handout MG.1) is located in the "Handouts" section near the end of this manual.

Using the Video with Chapter 13

With this video, you can provide an opportunity for students to critique a science teacher's use of questions, expository instruction, and demonstration techniques.

Before you begin: Distribute the handout. Explain that students should use it to take notes about the lesson they observe. Briefly describe the specific criteria listed on the handout:

Attitudes: What attitudes does the teacher display for his students and for the subject matter?
  Warmth and Empathy: Does the teacher convey caring and concern for his students?
  High Expectations: Does the teacher expect students to learn and achieve at a high level?
  Enthusiasm and Energy: Is the teacher enthusiastic about the topic he is discussing?
  Modeling: Does the teacher model his interest and enthusiasm for his students?
Organization: Is the teacher well organized? Does each topic flow logically from the preceding one?
Communication: How clearly and effectively is the teacher communicating ideas?
  Precise Terminology: Is he defining his terms precisely?
  Connected Discourse: How easily can one follow his train of thought?
  Transition Signals: Does he let students know when he is switching from one topic to another?
  Emphasis: Does he emphasize important ideas?

<u>Focus</u>: How well does the teacher focus students' attention?

  <u>Introductory Focus</u>: Does he make his objectives clear at the beginning of the lesson?

  <u>Sensory Focus</u>: Does he use techniques that are likely to keep students' eyes and ears focused on him?

  <u>Academic Focus</u>: Does he keep the class discussion focused on his objectives?

<u>Feedback</u>: Does he provide clear and immediate feedback about students' responses?

<u>Monitoring</u>: Does he check for students' understanding of the material?

<u>Questioning</u>: What questions does the teacher ask?

  <u>Frequency</u>: How often does he ask questions?

  <u>Equitable Distribution</u>: Does he call on some students more than on others? (For example, does he call on one gender more frequently than the other?)

  <u>Prompting</u>: Does he give hints when students don't initially know an answer?

  <u>Wait Time</u>: How much wait time does he allow after his questions? How much wait time does he allow after students' responses?

  <u>Question Level</u>: What lower-level questions does he ask? What higher-level questions does he ask?

<u>Review and Closure</u>: Does he effectively bring the lesson to a close? If so, how?

After the video: You may wish to ask questions such as these:

- <u>Which of the "essential teaching skills" are evident in the lesson, and how?</u>
  Discussion should focus on the specific criteria identified in the video and the handout.

- <u>The teacher uses a ribbon to show the length of a tapeworm (20 meters) in a human being. Is this strategy effective? If so, why?</u>
  The ribbon provides a concrete illustration of how long a single tapeworm can be. The tapeworm's length is surprisingly long for the place (intestines) in which it resides. To put it in the teacher's words, "If that does not sound gross, I don't know what gross is."

- <u>At the end of the class session, the teacher asks students to review today's lesson. He then briefly describes the next day's lesson. What advantages do the review and preview have?</u>
  The review enables students to identify the main ideas of the lesson, and it enables the teacher to check for students' understanding of the topics that were discussed. In his preview of the next lesson (dealing with the liver fluke), the teacher draws a connection between today's topic and the following one.

Educational Psychology Video Package, Video II: Segment #4

INVOLVING STUDENTS THROUGH GROUP WORK

Brief Description: This segment illustrates three possible uses of cooperative learning: (1) to facilitate review, (2) to teach study skills, and (3) to teach complex cognitive processes. In the first episode, sixth graders review a science lesson in cooperative groups; their teacher gives them a choice about how to proceed but provides guidance to groups who seem to flounder. In the second episode, a junior high school science teacher asks students to develop a mnemonic (a superimposed meaningful structure—in particular, a story) to help them remember the life cycle of a sheep liver fluke. In the third episode, the same science teacher encourages higher-level thinking and problem solving by asking groups to consider how they might stop flukes from progressing from each stage of development to the next.

Relevant Chapters: Chapters 8 and 13

Duration: The entire segment lasts approximately 16 minutes. The first and second episodes are 5 minutes each. The third episode is 6 minutes.

Location: The segment begins approximately one hour and $6^1/_2$ minutes into the video.

Using the Video with Chapter 8

You can use Episode 2 to illustrate how cooperative groups can promote an effective study strategy (developing and using mnemonics). You can use Episode 3 to illustrate how cooperative groups can facilitate complex problem solving.

Before you begin the second episode (mnemonics): Explain that developing sophisticated study strategies is often a challenging task. Cooperative groups provide one form of scaffolding in this endeavor.

After the second episode: You may wish to ask questions such as these:
- How does the teacher scaffold the students' review?
  She gives them a list of questions that they should be able to answer.
- Why might a group review be a valuable experience at the sixth-grade level?
  Students at this grade level have not yet developed many effective study strategies.
  Group work is one way of making a difficult task easier for these students.

Before you begin the third episode (problem solving): Explain that cooperative groups serve as a source of scaffolding that support students' attempts to solve difficult problems. Furthermore, a cooperative group provides an opportunity for students to verbalize their problem-solving strategies, and therefore to serve as models for one another regarding alternative strategies.

After the third episode: You may wish to ask such questions as these:

- <u>What's the advantage of having students develop a mnemonic as a group rather than individually?</u>
  They are likely to generate more creative ideas as a group than any one of them could generate independently.

- <u>What other study strategies might students be able to practice in a group situation?</u>
  Virtually any study strategy—elaborating, summarizing, taking notes, etc.—can be used in a group context as well as in an individual one.

Using the Video with Chapter 13

You can use all three episodes together to illustrate some of the many purposes that cooperative learning groups might serve.

Before you begin: Ask students to brainstorm potential advantages of cooperative learning. Building on their responses, explain that cooperative groups can be used for multiple purposes, including three that the video will illustrate: (1) facilitating review, (2) teaching study skills, and (3) teaching problem-solving.

During the video: Stop the video tape after the first episode and ask:

- <u>How does the teacher scaffold the students' review?</u>
  She gives them a list of questions that they should be able to answer.

- <u>Why might a group review be a valuable experience at the sixth-grade level?</u>
  Students at this grade level have not yet developed many effective learning and study strategies (see Chapters 2 and 8 in the textbook). Group work is one way of making a difficult task easier for these students.

Stop the video after the second episode and ask:

- <u>What's the advantage of having students develop a mnemonic as a group rather than individually?</u>
  They are likely to generate more creative mnemonics as a group than any one of them could generate independently.

- <u>Are the cooperative groups heterogeneous?</u>
  Not necessarily. Groups are formed based on where students are sitting in the classroom; if friends are sitting near one another, they might all be in the same group. We see at least one group composed entirely of girls.

After the video: You may wish to ask questions such as these:

- <u>What evidence do we see that the task of identifying ways to interrupt the fluke's life cycle is a difficult one for the students?</u>
  They ask a lot of questions and need considerable teacher guidance to proceed.

- <u>Based on the three examples of cooperative learning we've just observed, what are some possible advantages of cooperative learning?</u>
  Advantages evident in the film are these:
  - Students scaffold one another's performance on a difficult task.
  - Students must express their thoughts aloud and can therefore model their mental processes for one another.
  - Students can help one another monitor their comprehension.

Educational Psychology Video Package, Video II: Segment #5

TEACHING WHOLE LANGUAGE

Brief Description: A first-grade teacher reads a book about one child's favorite food, a peanut butter and jelly sandwich. Following the story, she has students complete three activities: (1) drawing a picture of their favorite food and writing a sentence about the picture, (2) putting sentences from the story in correct order, and (3) writing a story about their favorite sandwich.

Relevant Chapter: "Learning in the Content Areas"

Duration: The segment lasts approximately 11 minutes.

Location: The segment begins approximately one hour and 24 minutes into the video.

Using the Video with "Learning in the Content Areas"

You can use the video to illustrate whole language instruction and to foreshadow ideas that students will later encounter in Chapters 12 and 14.

Before you begin: Explain the rationale underlying whole language instruction—that it integrates various aspects of written and oral communication (reading, writing, spelling, speaking, etc.) into natural, real-life activities. (For example, reading is often taught using newspaper articles, storybooks, and other "natural" reading material rather than with a relatively structured classroom reading series.)

After the video: You may wish to ask questions such as these:
- How does the teacher activate students' prior knowledge before she reads the story?
    She asks, "How many of you have favorite foods?"
- When the teacher reads the storybook at the front of the room, she asks the students to read the sentence "But peanut butter and jelly is my favorite thing to eat" as she reaches the bottom of each page. It's possible that some of the children can't read all the words and are simply reciting the sentence from memory each time. What advantage might there be in having children recite something that they cannot necessarily read?
    It promotes knowledge related to *emergent* literacy—for instance, the awareness that certain combinations of symbols on the page stand for certain words in spoken language, and the knowledge that reading proceeds from the top of the page to the bottom.
- After the story, the teacher asks the students to draw a picture of their favorite food and to write a story about their favorite sandwich. What purposes might these activities serve?
    The activities should encourage the children to relate literature to their own lives. The writing activity also gives students a chance to practice basic writing skills within the context of an authentic writing task.

- <u>The teacher gives the students individual sentence strips from the story and asks them to arrange them in the correct order. What purpose might this activity serve?</u>
  If students know the story quite well, they might be able to recite the book from memory rather than actually read the words on the page. But to accomplish the sentence-strip task, they must actually read the sentences. They do not necessarily have to decipher every word, but they need to recognize enough of the words in each sentence to get its gist and determine where the sentence appears in the story.

- <u>What advantages and disadvantages might whole language instruction have in comparison with a more traditional, basic-skills approach?</u>
  Students can more easily relate (and transfer) newly acquired language skills to one another and to the world in which they must eventually use the skills. However, some important reading and/or writing skills may not be taught in a sufficiently systematic fashion to promote mastery. (You and your students may identify other advantages and disadvantages as well.)

- (to foreshadow issues in Chapters 12 and 14) <u>What strategies does the teacher use to keep students motivated and on task?</u>
  - She keeps the students consistently and actively engaged in classroom tasks.
  - She relates reading and writing to students' own lives.
  - She models interest in the subject matter.
  - She gives students a choice regarding the topic they write about.
  - She gives competence-promoting feedback.
  - In one instance, she scaffolds a difficult task. When a student tries to write the word *bread*, she makes a "br" sound that tells the student what the first letters must be. She then tells the girl the last three letters ("e, a, d").
  (You and your students may identify other strategies as well.)

Observing Children and Adolescents in Classroom Settings: Observation #1

PORTFOLIO

Brief Description: A student named Keenan reviews her work samples with her second-grade teacher. They compare her present performance in spelling, grammar, and reading with her performance in kindergarten and first grade.

Relevant Chapters: Chapters 12, 15, 16, and the chapter "Learning in the Content Areas" (the last of these chapters is on the Companion Website and in the *Study Guide and Reader*)

Duration: The video segment lasts approximately 5 minutes.

Location: The segment begins approximately 45 seconds into the video.

Accompanying Materials: Three Observation Records (Handouts MG.2, MG.3, and MG.4) are located in the "Handouts" section near the end of this manual.

Using the Video with Chapter 12

The video offers several examples of intrinsic motivation and self-regulation (hence, it also draws from the discussion of self-regulation in Chapter 10). In addition, the video illustrates strategies for promoting motivation through self-assessment.

Before you begin: Provide a brief review of the concepts of *intrinsic motivation* and *self-regulation*:
- *Intrinsic motivation:* An internal desire to perform a particular task
- *Self-regulation:* Setting standards and goals for oneself and engaging in behaviors that lead to their accomplishment

Explain that the video shows a second grader (Keenan) and her teacher reviewing Keenan's progress in writing and reading over the past two years.

Distribute Handout MG.2 (Observation Record for "Portfolio" — Motivation and Self-Regulation) and review the questions that your students should consider as they watch Keenan and her teacher.

After the video: Ask your students to share their analyses related to each of the questions on the Observation Record. Some possible responses to the questions are as follows:

What the *Student* Is Doing	
Look for...	Record Your Observations of the Student
Intrinsic Motivation What does the student do and say to indicate that she is intrinsically motivated to read and write?	She acknowledges her errors and doesn't seem embarrassed by them (e.g., she says that the arrows in her story mean that she needs to indent more), suggesting that she has a mastery goal rather than a performance goal. When she doesn't know how to spell a word, she asks a friend or her teacher. This, again, suggests a mastery goal; it also indicates that she believes that success is within her control (an internal, controllable attribution). She seems proud about the fact that she reads lengthy books (e.g., she says that she has already spent three days reading *A Frog's Body*). She says that she enjoys reading books about animals.
Self-Regulation What behaviors and/or statements indicate that the student is acquiring some self-regulatory strategies related to her reading and writing?	She seeks help when she needs it. She makes notations to remind herself about where she needs to make changes in her work (i.e., she draws arrows to indicate where she needs to indent). She is engaging in self-evaluation. She reads independently.

What the *Teacher* Is Doing	
Look for...	Record Your Observations of the Teacher
Motivational Strategies What strategies is the teacher using to motivate the student?	The teacher focuses the student's attention on her improvement over time. She praises the student (e.g., saying, "That's great!" when the student says that she now knows how to use an ellipsis). She focuses the student's attention on the internal pleasure that her accomplishments bring (i.e., she says, "You should be proud"). In general, she communicates affection and a genuine interest in the student's progress.

Following are additional questions you may want to ask at the end of the videotape:

- One of the strategies that Keenan's teacher uses is praise. Praise can promote either extrinsic or intrinsic motivation, depending on the message that it gives. Under what circumstances is praise most likely to promote *intrinsic* motivation?

  It is most likely to do so when it communicates high competence (e.g., "You're really good at this kind of thing") and maintains students' sense of self-determination (e.g., "You seem to have learned some very effective study strategies"). Praise is *unlikely* to promote intrinsic motivation when it communicates low competence (e.g., when students are praised for doing something very easy) or when it undermines their sense of self-determination (e.g., "Good, you did what I asked you to do").

- What other strategies does the textbook identify for promoting intrinsic motivation?

  This question should encourage students to review what they have read in Chapter 12. Responses should focus on *intrinsic* rather than extrinsic motivation; following are several examples:

  - Define success as eventual, rather than immediate, mastery of a topic or skill.
  - Enhance students' self-efficacy and sense of competence by helping them be successful at school tasks.
  - Present situations about which students are naturally curious and interested.
  - Show how school subject matter has relevance for students' own lives.
  - Create disequilibrium by presenting surprising information or phenomena.
  - Promote a sense of self-determination (e.g., by offering choices).
  - Encourage a focus on mastery goals.
  - Communicate the fact that occasional mistakes and failures are inevitable, and make allowances for such mistakes and failures when assigning grades.

- Focus students' attention on their own progress, rather than on how their performance compares to that of their classmates.
- Show students that they have control over what happens to them (i.e., foster internal attributions).

- <u>What strategies does the textbook identify for promoting self-regulation?</u>
  This question should encourage review of the material in Chapter 10. Following are examples of possible responses:
  - Teach self-regulatory strategies (e.g., self-instructions, self-monitoring, self-evaluation, self-reinforcement).
  - Model self-regulating behaviors.
  - Provide age-appropriate opportunities for independence.
  - Offer help only when students really need it.

Using the Video with Chapter 15 or 16

You can use the video to illustrate how a teacher might use a portfolio to engage students in self-evaluation, with a focus on their own improvement over time.

Before you begin: Provide a brief description of a *portfolio*—in particular, that it is a systematic collection of a student's work over a lengthy period, and that students are actively involved in its development and evaluation. Distribute Handout MG.3 (Observation Record for "Portfolio"—Self-Assessment) and review the questions that your students should consider as they watch the video.

After the video: Ask your students to share their analyses related to each of the questions on the Observation Record. Some possible responses to the questions are as follows:

What the *Student* Is Doing	
Look for...	Record Your Observations of the Student
Self-Assessment What improvements does the student identify in her writing and reading?	**In writing:** She is more knowledgeable about paragraphs and the need to indent at the beginning of each one. She is more knowledgeable about punctuation (ellipsis, period, comma, apostrophe) and capitalization rules. She knows how to spell more words. She has learned how to use the dictionary to find word spellings.

In reading:

She reads smaller print.

The books she reads have longer, more complex sentences.

She reads longer books and is now beginning to read chapter books.

She recognizes more words.

She has begun to read independently.

What the *Teacher* Is Doing	
Look for...	Record Your Observations of the Teacher
Teaching Strategies In what ways does the teacher scaffold the student's efforts to evaluate her own progress?	She facilitates comparisons by putting two things (two writing samples, two reading books) side by side. She focuses the student's attention on particular features (e.g., "I notice here that you're starting to write paragraphs"; "Is there any difference in the stories [the student has read in kindergarten and in second grade]?"). She helps to clarify what the student is trying to say (e.g., "That shows me, now you know how to use an ellipsis, and you didn't before"; "You were confused on what an apostrophe was, and a comma. Now you know the difference"). She encourages the student to think about how her strategies have changed ("What did you do when you came up to a word you didn't know how to spell?"). She encourages the student to appreciate her progress ("You should be proud").

Using the Video with "Learning in the Content Areas"

You can use the video to illustrate developmental changes in students' reading and writing skills in the primary grades.

Before you begin: Explain that a teacher and a second-grader named Keenan are looking at how Keenan's reading and writing skills have changed over the past two years. Distribute Handout MG.4 (Observation Record for "Portfolio"— Literacy Development) and review the questions that your students should consider as they watch the video.

After the video: Ask your students to share their analyses related to each of the questions on the Observation Record. Some possible responses to the questions are as follows:

What the *Student* Is Doing	
Look for...	Record Your Observations of the Student
Writing Development What developmental changes do you see in the student's writing?	She is more knowledgeable about paragraphs and the need to indent at the beginning of each one. She is more knowledgeable about punctuation (ellipsis, period, comma, apostrophe) and capitalization rules. She knows how to spell more words. She has learned how to use the dictionary to find word spellings. Her stories are longer. Her handwriting is smaller and more controlled.
Reading Development What developmental changes do you see in the student's reading?	She reads smaller print. The books she reads have longer, more complex sentences. She reads longer books and is now beginning to read chapter books. She has a larger reading vocabulary. She has begun to read independently.

Following is an additional question you may want to ask at the end of the videotape:

- <u>As a second grader, does Keenan have any knowledge or skills that seem advanced for her age?</u>

  Responses to this question are likely to vary. It appears that Keenan is somewhat advanced in her knowledge of punctuation; for instance, she has some knowledge of when an ellipsis (. . .) should be used. Furthermore, Keenan is beginning to read chapter books (e.g., the *Babysitters' Club* series) independently. You might point out that behaviors that appear "advanced" in one group of children may be only "average" in another group of the same age; children's cultural backgrounds and prior literacy experiences at home will play a key role in what is "typical" for a particular population.

Observing Children and Adolescents in Classroom Settings: Observation #2

PAINTING CLASS

Brief Description: An elementary school student, Paula, is being interviewed while painting a landscape scene. She and her classmates have been learning about Monet and other impressionists and the techniques that these artists used.

Relevant Chapter: Chapter 16

Duration: The video segment lasts approximately 2 minutes.

Location: The segment begins approximately 6 minutes into the video.

Accompanying Materials: An Observation Record (Handout MG.5) is located in the "Handouts" section near the end of this manual.

Using the Video with Chapter 16

You can use the video to stimulate discussion about *informal assessment*—in particular, about the kinds of teacher questions that are and are not likely to provide helpful information about students' learning and understanding.

Before you begin: Explain that an elementary student is being interviewed about what she is doing and learning in her art class. Ask students to listen to the kinds of questions the interviewer asks and the kinds of information she does and does not get as a result of her questions.

Distribute Handout MG.5 (Observation Record for "Painting Class") and review the questions that your students should consider as they listen to both the child and the interviewer.

After the video: Ask your students to share their analyses related to each of the questions on the Observation Record. Some possible responses to the questions are as follows:

What Questions the *Interviewer* Is Asking	
Look for...	Record Examples of Questions the Interviewer Asks
Kinds of questions What kinds of questions does the interviewer ask?	The interviewer asks only very general questions about what Paula and her classmates are doing and what they have learned. The following questions illustrate: • "Can you tell me what you're working on?" • "What are you doing exactly on your painting? What part are you working on right now?" • "Are you having fun?" • "Is this a good project, and what are you learning?" • "What have you learned so far?" • "What did [Monet] paint?"

What Information the *Student* Is Providing	
Look for...	Record Examples of the Student's Responses to Questions
Student's responses What kinds of information is the student providing? What kinds of information is she *not* providing?	Paula's responses describe what she's learned at only a superficial level. We learn little if anything about her true understanding of, or appreciation for, impressionist art. The following responses illustrate: • "We're making our own impressionist's paintings, because we're studying Monet, a French impressionist painter." • "I'm working on the grass, we're... and we're doing like a meadow, and a hill, and the sky, with flowers. And right now we're working on the grass and the mountains." • "Yeah, we're working on the background." • "We're learning about Monet." • "We've learned about where he lived and what he painted." In response to the question, "What did he paint?", she responds, "Impressionist paintings." • "He painted the scenes outside and different...different light and what it looked like."

Following are additional questions you may want to ask at the end of the videotape:

- <u>Do we have any evidence that Paula has a meaningful understanding of impressionists and their work?</u>

    Paula does understand that impressionists tried to capture the effects of light, but most of her responses reflect little more than rote learning (e.g., Monet painted "impressionist paintings"). It is quite possible that Paula has learned a great deal more than she shows in the interview. Unfortunately, the interviewer does not follow up with more specific and directive questions to probe Paula's understanding and reasoning.

- <u>What kinds of questions might the interviewer have asked to get a better assessment of what Paula has learned in the unit on impressionism?</u>

    Your students are likely to have many creative ideas. Following are a few possibilities:

    - "How might you recognize an impressionist painting if you saw one in an art museum?"
    - "What things are you doing in your own painting that are similar to techniques that Monet used?"
    - "What kinds of things did Monet paint? Why did he pick those particular things?"

Observing Children and Adolescents in Classroom Settings: Observation #3

PIAGET TASKS

Brief Description: A woman presents four Piagetian tasks that assess conservation of quantity, liquid, and number: (a) a comparison of pizza divided into four versus eight pieces, (b) a comparison of two balls of clay (one of which is smashed into a pancake shape), (c) a comparison of water in two different sized beakers, and (d) a comparison of two rows of six pennies each (one of which is spread out so that it is longer than the other). Both preoperational and concrete operational reasoning are depicted.

Relevant Chapter: Chapter 2

Duration: The video segment lasts approximately $6^1/_2$ minutes.

Location: The segment begins approximately 8 minutes into the video.

Accompanying Materials: An Observation Record (Handout MG.6) is located in the "Handouts" section near the end of this manual.

Using the Video with Chapter 2

You can use the video to help your students distinguish between preoperational and concrete operational thinking. You can also use it to give your students a chance to observe and evaluate a teacher's use of Piaget's clinical method.

Before you begin: Give an overview of Piaget's preoperational and concrete operational stages, explaining that conservation is one acquisition that marks the onset of concrete operations. Also describe Piaget's clinical method, explaining that ideally, the interviewer asks a variety of questions to thoroughly assess how a child is reasoning about a situation. As an example, you might refer to the series of questions in "Poppies and Bluebells," an Interpreting Artifacts and Interactions feature in Chapter 2.

Distribute Handout MG.6 (Observation Record for "Piaget Tasks") and review the questions that your students should consider as they watch both the children and the teacher.

After the video: Ask your students to share their analyses related to each of the questions on the Observation Record. Some possible responses to the questions are as follows:

What the *Students* Are Doing	
Look for...	Record Your Observations of the Students
Preoperational Thought What statements reflect preoperational thinking?	A boys sees nothing wrong in someone saying that a pizza cut into four pieces would be better than a pizza cut into eight pieces because eight pieces would be too much to eat. A girl says that one lump of clay has more "because it's flattened out like a pancake." A girl says the thinner beaker has more water because it is "taller." A boy says that two rows of six pennies are different after one row has been spread out.
Concrete Operational Thought What statements reflect concrete operational thinking?	A girl realizes that two pizzas cut into four and eight pieces, respectively, are equivalent. A boy and a girl say that a flattened ball of clay still has the same amount of clay as a similar, nonflattened ball. A girl recognizes that water doesn't change in amount just because it's poured into a wider beaker. A girl realizes that two rows of six pennies each have the same amount of pennies. "One of them is just spread out more," she explains.
What the *Teacher* Is Doing	
Look for...	Record Your Observations of the Teacher
Conservation Tasks What specific tasks does the teacher present to assess the students' understanding of conservation?	Cutting a pizza (depicted on a sheet of paper) into four versus eight pieces Forming two balls of clay and then flattening one ball into pancake Pouring water into similar beakers and then transferring the water from one of the beakers into a wider beaker Comparing rows of pennies that are close together versus far apart

Use of Clinical Method What kinds of questions does the teacher ask? Does she ask enough questions to get a full understanding of the students' reasoning?	The teacher asks students to compare quantities, but she does not always ask enough questions to get a full understanding of the students' reasoning, nor does she present any information that might challenge their reasoning. Following are two examples: • In the conservation of liquid task, she asks if the two differently shaped beakers have the same amount of water. A girl responds, "That one's taller." The teacher does not ask any follow-up questions to determine whether "taller" also means different in amount. She might have pointed out that the water in the taller beaker is also "wider" to see how the child responded. • When comparing two rows of pennies, a boy says, "They're different, because that one's smaller and that one's bigger." The teacher asks, "Why?" and he responds "Because you spread them out." We still do not know, however, whether he believes that "different" and "spread out" are equivalent to *more* pennies. She might have pointed out that each row has six pennies and asked, "Do you still think mine has more? If so, why?" Young children sometimes misinterpret what is being asked in Piaget's tasks.

Observing Children and Adolescents in Classroom Settings: Observation #4

DESIGNING EXPERIMENTS

Brief Description: This video segment presents several excerpts from the Merrill video *Insights into Learning: Designing Experiments in Seventh Grade*. At the beginning of the video, a seventh-grade science teacher explains the assignment for the day: to determine what factor(s) affect a pendulum's swing. The video then focuses on a group of four students who are testing effects of weight, length, and angle (i.e., height from which the pendulum is dropped). The students initially confound weight and length. Gradually, through a series of questions, the teacher nudges them toward the realization that they must test each variable separately.

Relevant Chapter: Chapter 2

Duration: The video segment lasts approximately 9 minutes.

Location: The segment begins approximately 14 minutes into the video.

Accompanying Materials: An Observation Record (Handout MG.7) is located in the "Handouts" section near the end of this manual.

Using the Video with Chapter 2

You can use the video to illustrate concrete operational and formal operational reasoning, as well as instructional strategies for encouraging the separation and control of variables.

Before you begin: Introduce the video as an illustration of how seventh graders are likely to approach a task requiring separation and control of variables. In the video, a science teacher has students work in small groups to test three variables that might affect a pendulum's oscillation weight: length, weight, and height (the teacher uses the term *angle*) from which the pendulum is dropped. Earlier in the school year, students have had formal instruction about the importance of separating and controlling variables; they have also conducted a structured experiment in which they tested the effects of fertilizer, light source, and temperature on plant growth.

Distribute Handout MG.7 (Observation Record for "Designing Experiments") and review the questions that your students should consider as they watch both the children and the teacher. Point out that the groups are using large paperclips to add weight to their pendulums.

After the video: Ask your students to share their analyses related to each of the questions on the Observation Record. Some possible responses to the questions are as follows:

What the *Students* Are Doing	
Look for...	Record Your Observations of the Students
Concrete Operations What behaviors and statements reflect concrete operational thinking?	The students change all three variables—weight, length, and height—between test 1 and test 2. Marina says, "We found out that the shorter it is and the heavier it is, the faster it goes." Even after students realize that they must keep two variables constant while testing the third variable, they simultaneously increase both weight and length by adding each additional paperclip *at the bottom of* the other paperclip(s). At the end of the video, Marina says, "And the second one was ...the height was ... it was higher, but the weight was lower, so it's the same thing."
Formal Operations What behaviors and statements reflect formal operational thinking?	After some guiding questions from the teacher, the group begins to hold two variables constant while testing the third. After comparing a test the group has just conducted with the preceding test, Paige says, "It's the same height, same paperclips. It's just the length is different."

What the *Teacher* Is Doing	
Look for...	Record Your Observations of the Teacher
Scaffolding In what ways does the teacher scaffold the students' reasoning?	At the beginning of the lesson, the teacher suggests three variables that might affect a pendulum's swing. The teacher asks numerous probing questions to get the group to reflect on how it has failed to separate and control variables. Following are some examples: "What did you change ... between test 1 and test 2? ... So you changed the weight. What else did you change? ... And so you changed all three between the two tests.... Which caused that higher frequency? ... Why can't you all come to a conclusion by looking at the numbers?" "What was the first thing you said?" (Marina says, "Everything changed.") "Okay, think about that." He focuses students' attention on what they are doing when they add each new paperclip to the bottom of the lowest paperclip: "Look at that system and tell me how you could be making a slight mistake with weight and length.... What are you changing also when you change the weight by doing that? How can you change that? How can you make that better? ... Can you think of a way to redesign it so that you're only changing the weight? ... How can you change it so it won't get longer when you add the paperclip?"
Types of Feedback What kinds of feedback does the teacher give the students about their performance?	The teacher never specifically tells the students that they are right or wrong. Instead, his questions encourage the students to reflect about the validity of their own actions.

Following are additional questions to ask at the end of the videotape:

- <u>How much scaffolding do these seventh graders need to separate and control variables successfully?</u>

   They require quite a bit of scaffolding. Even so, at least one student (Marina) does not appear to completely understand the importance of separating and controlling variables (e.g., as indicated by her statement near the end of lesson that "the height was ... it was higher, but the weight was lower, so it's the same thing").

- <u>From Piaget's perspective, would you expect seventh graders to be able to separate and control variables?</u>

   According to Piaget, the ability to separate and control variables appears in the formal operations stage, which, on average, emerges at around 11 or 12 years of age. Many seventh graders would still be making the transition from concrete to formal operational thought and so may not have mastered the ability to separate and control variables.

Observing Children and Adolescents in Classroom Settings: Observation #5

PENDULUM PRESENTATION

Brief Description: Five elementary school students have just completed an experiment to test the effect of weight on a pendulum's oscillation rate. The students are now presenting their findings and conclusions to their teacher and classmates. The students have clearly been unable to separate and control variables, and they have erroneously concluded that weight affects a pendulum's swing.

Relevant Chapter: Chapter 2

Duration: The video segment lasts approximately $4^1/_2$ minutes.

Location: The segment begins approximately 23 minutes into the video.

Accompanying Material: An Observation Record (Handout MG.8) is located in the "Handouts" section near the end of this manual.

Using the Video with Chapter 2

You can use the video to give your students the opportunity to analyze children's scientific reasoning processes and evaluate a teacher's attempts to encourage separation and control of variables.

Before you begin: Explain that the children have been working in small groups ("pods") to conduct pendulum experiments using washers of various sizes. Each group began with a *posing question* that guided its subsequent experimentation; each group also created a poster that summarized its findings and conclusions. One group of five children generated the posing question: "What size washer would swing the most in 15 seconds?" The children are now presenting their results to the rest of the class.

Distribute Handout MG.8 (Observation Record for "Pendulum Presentation") and review the questions that your students should consider as they watch both the children and the teacher. You might play the video twice, asking your students to consider what the *children* are doing the first time through and what the *teacher* is doing the second time through.

After the video: Ask your students to share their analyses related to each of the questions on the Observation Record. Some possible responses to the questions are as follows:

What the *Students* Are Doing	
Look for...	Record Your Observations of the Students
Concrete Operations What statements reflect concrete operational thinking?	The three group members who speak all assert that weight affects a pendulum's swing, when in reality weight does *not* make a difference. Their "finding" suggests that they did not systematically separate and control variables during their experimentation.
Formal Operations What statements reflect formal operational thinking?	One girl asks whether the group members kept the length of the string constant when testing the effect of weight. Later, another girl suggests that the group test its "wind" hypothesis by swinging a pendulum in both windy and nonwindy conditions. (Although this suggestion does not specifically address the need to separate and control variables, it does at least indicate the need to test the hypothesis systematically.)
What the *Teacher* Is Doing	
Look for...	Record Your Observations of the Teacher
Scaffolding In what ways does the teacher scaffold the students' reasoning?	She suggests that each group identify a posing question to guide its experimentation efforts. She asks the students how they might set up experiments to test particular hypotheses. She points out that two different groups reached opposite conclusions about the effect of weight and asks students to consider what scientists do when they get conflicting results. She asks, "How would you set up an experiment to prove that, or disprove that? Anyone have a suggestion how they might be able to set up a more controlled experiment to see what would happen?"
Type of Feedback What kinds of feedback does the teacher give the students about their performance?	She points out that the presenting group has obtained a result in direct contradiction to the results of another group. She tells the two groups that have gotten conflicting results, "Everybody's answers are correct because you saw it, you observed it, so this is your evidence." On two occasions, she says, "Good job," but does not explain which aspects of their performance to which she is referring.

Following are additional questions to ask at the end of the videotape:

- The group's posing question was, "What size washer would swing the most in 15 seconds?" How might their question have biased their experimentation and observations? Rather than asking *whether* weight makes a difference, the group asked *how* weight makes a difference, thereby increasing the likelihood that the children would "see" differences in oscillation rate that didn't necessarily exist.

- What specific conclusion has the presenting group reached about the effect of weight? A pendulum with a medium weight swings the fastest (i.e., one that's "not too heavy, not too light"). The group reports that in a 15-second interval, the medium weight swung 14 times, the large one swung 13 times, the small one swung 10 times.

- What explanations do the group members provide for the weight's effects? The three boys who speak offer several explanations:
  - "The bigger the washer was, the more swings there were, 'cause there's more pull on it."
  - "There's no traction going up and down" (for the small washer).
  - "The medium gets more speed, because it's not too heavy and its not too small and light, and it got just enough speed so it got more counts."
  - "The bigger one, it went slower because the wind stopped it more, and it had to take longer time to get back and forth. But the smallest one, it made such little ones, and it was so slow that it didn't do enough. But the medium one, there wasn't a lot of wind stopping it and it was still pretty heavy.... The wind has to do with it, like the wind stops it.... I mean the air."
  - "The little one, the string weighed more than the small one [sic], it might have held it up more.... The string might weigh more than the little washer."

- What does the teacher do/say that might lead the children in the presenting group to erroneously believe that their conclusion is correct? She says and does several things::
  - She says, "Everybody's answers are correct because you saw it, you observed it, so this is your evidence."
  - She says, "Good job," and claps.
  - Later she again says, "Good job, guys."
  - She ends the lesson with some of the children still believing that weight makes a difference.

- If you had been the teacher, what would you have done differently? Following are three of the many possible responses to this question:
  - Ask all five members of the group to give their own interpretations of their findings. Only three of the five group members—all of them boys—describe the group's findings and conclusions. These three offer differing explanations for how weight supposedly affected the pendulum's swing.
  - Place greater emphasis on the fact that two groups found conflicting results about the possible effects of weight. Rather than gloss over the discrepancy (e.g., by saying "Everybody's answers are correct because you saw it, you observed it"), get the children involved in follow-up experimentation to bring resolution to the matter.
  - Form new groups that are heterogeneous with respect to beliefs about the effect of weight; that is, each group should include at least one child who thinks that weight makes a difference and at least one child who does *not*. Ask the groups to conduct additional experiments to test the effect of weight. Because of the differing opinions going into the process, group discussions are more likely to create *disequilibrium* for some or all of the group members.

Observing Children and Adolescents in Classroom Settings: Observation #6

BIRDWATCHING

Brief Description: Several young children visit a nature center, where they observe and learn about birds in their local area.

Relevant Chapter: Chapter 2

Duration: The video segment lasts approximately $1\frac{1}{2}$ minutes.

Location: The segment begins approximately $27\frac{1}{2}$ minutes into the video.

Accompanying Materials: An Observation Record (Handout MG.9) is located in the "Handouts" section near the end of this manual.

Using the Video with Chapter 2

You can use this video to illustrate children's constructive, meaning-making processes, as well as Vygotsky's sociocultural perspective of education.

Before you begin: Explain that several young children are visiting a local nature center, where a wildlife specialist is helping them observe and learn about birds. Distribute Handout MG.9 (Observation Record for "Birdwatching") and review the questions that your students should consider as they watch both the children and the adult. Because the video is short, you may want to show the video twice, asking your students to consider what the *children* are doing the first time through and what the *adult* is doing the second time through.

After the video: Ask your students to share their analyses related to each of the questions on the Observation Record. Some possible responses to the questions are as follows:

What the *Children* Are Doing	
Look for...	Record Your Observations of the Children
Interactions with the physical environment In what ways do the children interact with their physical environment?	The children are observing the behavior of birds at a birdfeeder. One boy is learning about the effect of binoculars. He looks through them at a girl's hair and remarks, "Your hair is golden." Then he says to her, "Could you turn around again? I can see your eyes." The children open the kinds of seeds that the birds are eating. For example, Sean opens one and discovers "white stuff" inside.

Construction of meaning What understandings do the children construct during the activity?	One child incorrectly labels a birdfeeder as a birdhouse, showing assimilation to a "birdhouse" scheme. The children appear to be getting a better understanding of what the seeds are like. As the children are looking at a picture of several birds, Kent draws an analogy: "Instead of hands, they have wings."
What the *Adult* Is Doing	
Look for...	Record Your Observations of the Adult
Scaffolding In what ways does the adult scaffold the children's learning?	She suggests how Sean might further dissect his seed. She directs the children's attention to particular features of the birds in the picture.
Cultural interpretation At what points does the adult pass along her culture's interpretations of what the children are observing?	She tells them that the birdhouse is actually a birdfeeder. She points out the birds' sharp beaks and says, "I think they might make real good seed openers."

Following is an additional question to ask at the end of the videotape:

- In what ways are visits to nature centers, zoos, museums, and similar places likely to be beneficial for young children?
    Such visits are likely to expand children's knowledge about their world, thereby helping them more effectively and accurately interpret future experiences and school subject matter. (You might mention that students will learn more about the influence of prior knowledge in the discussion of cognitive processes in Chapters 6 and 7.)

Observing Children and Adolescents in Classroom Settings: Observation #7

BALANCE SCALES

Brief Description: A group of 4 fourth graders meets with educational psychologist Dr. Paul Eggen to discuss various solutions to balance scale problems.

Relevant Chapter: Chapter 8

Duration: The video segment lasts approximately 12 minutes.

Location: The segment begins approximately $29^1/_2$ minutes into the video.

Accompanying Materials: An Observation Record (Handout MG.10) and a transparency master (Transparency MG.8) are located, respectively, in the "Handouts" and "Transparency Masters" sections at the end of this manual.

Using the Video with Chapter 8

You can use this video to give students an opportunity to evaluate children's problem-solving strategies for balance scale problems within the context of Robert Siegler's theory. You may want to assign the simulation "Assessment in the Balance" on the CD *Simulations in Educational Psychology and Research* either before or after you show the video in class.

Before you begin: Show Part A of the transparency and explain the nature of balance scale problems: to put one or more weights on each side of the scale and make predictions about whether the scale will balance. Explain Siegler's proposal that, with age, children acquire increasingly sophisticated strategies for balance scale problems. More specifically, they tend to acquire the following three strategies as they grow older:

1. Initially, they consider only the amount of weight on each side of the scale. For example, they would predict that 10 grams placed on peg 3 on the left side would balance 10 grams placed on peg 7 on the right side.

2. Later, they begin to consider distance as well as weight and realize that weights placed farther out from the fulcrum have a greater effect than weights placed close to the fulcrum. However, they do not have a precise system for determining how distance compensates for weight. For example, they might predict that 20 grams placed on peg 3 on the left side would balance 10 grams placed on peg 7 on the right side.

3. Finally, they realize that weight and distance have a multiplicative relationship—that is, that the effect of weight is directly proportional to its distance from the fulcrum. For example, they would predict that 20 grams placed on peg 3 on the left side ($20 \times 3 = 60$) would balance 10 grams placed on peg 6 on the right side ($10 \times 6 = 60$). They also add multiple products on each side in reaching their conclusions. For example, they would predict that 20 grams placed on peg 3 on the left side ($20 \times 3 = 60$) would balance 10 grams on peg 5 and 5 grams on peg 2 on the right ($[10 \times 5] + [5 \times 2] = 60$). (Show Part B on the transparency to depict this solution.)

Explain that the video depicts 4 fourth graders—Drexel, Molly, Suzanne, and Tad—meeting with educational psychologist Paul Eggen to discuss various solutions to balance scale problems. Distribute Handout MG.10 (Observation Record for "Balance Scales") and ask students to look for solutions that appear to reflect each of Siegler's three balance scale strategies. Show Part C on the transparency and explain that this problem is the one that Dr. Eggen initially gives the children.

After the video: Ask your students to identify solutions that reflected each of the three strategies that Siegler describes. Below are examples of solutions in each category:

What the *Students* Are Doing	
Look for...	Record Your Observations of the Students
Siegler's Strategy 1 What responses consider only the number of weights on each side of the scale?	Tad: "If you put 4 on the 3 again, it will make it even because there's 4 on that side and there are 4 on that side, and that will make it balance, 'cause they got the same... *[Later]* Because there won't be too much on that side, too much on that side, so it will, like, balance. Well, it *should* balance." (Although Tad offers a correct solution, he appears to be considering only the number of weights on each side.) Suzanne: "I put 2 on the 5 over here *[adding to the left side]*, and then I put 2 on the 1 over here, 1 on the 2, and then 2 on the 9.... *[Part D of the transparency illustrates her solution.]* I think those will work, because if you count the blocks up, they'll equal up to the same thing, 'cause what I did is 2 + 3 = 5, and then 2 + 1 + 2 = 5." (Suzanne is thinking that there are initially 3 rather than 4 weights on peg 3 of the left side, so Dr. Eggen removes one of the weights.)
Siegler's Strategy 2 What responses consider distance as well as weight but without a precise understanding of how the two factors interrelate?	Molly: *(evaluating Suzanne's initial solution)* "It doesn't matter how many blocks there are, it's where they're put. Because if you have 2 on the 1 and 2 on the 4, it would be 8, and you'd be 2, and 8 and 2 don't equal up. (Molly recognizes that distance compensates for weight. Her calculations do include multiplication, but her reasoning isn't totally clear, leading me to categorize this response as Strategy 2 rather than Strategy 3.) Suzanne: "Maybe if you take 1 off the 9, it will work.... Because that's the farthest to the end, and sometimes it sort of matters because the ends kind of bring it down more." (Suzanne now recognizes that weights farther from the fulcrum have a greater effect than weights close to the fulcrum.)

Siegler's Strategy 3	Molly: "No. I figured it out. 5 and 5 is 10, and 3 X 3 is 9, 19. And 2 and 2 is 4.... Over there *[on the left]* they have 19, and over there they only have 4." *[Dr. Eggen asks, "Tell me how you got the 19?]* "3 x 3 = 9, and 5 X 2 = 10.... 15 needs to be put on that there *[on the right]*.... I think if you put 1 on the 10 and 1 on the 5, it should work."
What responses reflect a multiplicative relationship between number of weights and distance from the fulcrum?	Drexel: " So 2, plus 2 on the 1, are 4, and 4 plus 5 is 9, and 9 plus 10 is 19."

Observing Children and Adolescents in Classroom Settings: Observation #8

YEAST DISCUSSION

Brief Description: A middle school science class is looking at yeast under a microscope and discussing whether yeast is a form of life.

Relevant Chapter: Chapter 7 (the analysis of the video presented here also draws on the discussions of *cognitive apprenticeship* and *cognitive processes* in Chapters 2 and 6, respectively)

Duration: The video segment lasts approximately $1^1/_2$ minutes.

Location: The segment begins approximately $41^1/_2$ minutes into the video.

Accompanying Materials: An Observation Record (Handout MG.11) is located in the "Handouts" section near the end of this manual.

Using the Video with Chapter 7

You can use the video to have your students observe middle school students' personal theories about living things. The video also illustrates instructional strategies for promoting scientific reasoning, including elements of a cognitive apprenticeship.

Before you begin: Explain that a middle school science class has been studying the characteristics of living things. Today the class is looking at yeast under a microscope and discussing whether yeast is a living thing.

Distribute Handout MG.11 (Observation Record for "Yeast Discussion") and review the questions that your students should consider as they observe both the children and the teacher. Because the video is short, you may want to show the video twice, asking your students to consider what the *children* are doing the first time through and what the *teacher* is doing the second time through.

After the video: Ask your students to share their analyses related to each of the questions on the Observation Record. Some possible responses to the questions are as follows:

What the *Students* Are Doing	
Look for...	Record Your Observations of the Students
Children's Theories What do the students' comments tell us about their *personal theories* about the nature of life?	Chris says, "It's moving." Jessica says that she thinks she sees movement inside it, perhaps a beating heart. (We might wonder whether Jessica thinks that a beating heart is essential for all living beings; if so, this is a misconception that will need to be corrected.) Chris says, "He's adapting to his environment."
Cognitive Processes What behaviors indicate that the students are probably using effective cognitive processes?	The students appear to be paying close *attention* to the teacher, the yeast, and the class discussion. We do not see any students engaged in off-task behavior. The children are effectively using what they already know about living things to help them understand the nature of yeast; thus, they are engaging in *elaboration*.
What the *Teacher* Is Doing	
Look for...	Record Your Observations of the Teacher
Instructional Strategies What strategies does the teacher use to help the students understand the nature of yeast?	She asks them to consider the characteristics of living things (which they have previously learned) to determine if yeast is alive. She uses a series of questions to help them draw their own conclusions, and thereby to construct their own knowledge, about the nature of yeast.
Cognitive Apprenticeship What strategies does the teacher use to help the students think in ways that scientists think?	She models the use of a microscope. She uses the scientific term *organism* when referring to the yeast. She asks the students to substantiate their conclusions: "Can you give me a reason that you think he's alive?" "How do you know there's a little water?" She talks about making inferences from data: "From your experience before, when you looked in the microscope, you can infer that? That's a good inference."

Following is an additional question to ask at the end of the videotape:

- <u>How might a middle school student's theory about living things be different from a young child's theory about living things?</u>

    Young children often rely heavily on *movement* as a characteristic of living things, so much so that they sometimes infer that nonliving things (e.g., a truck, the wind) are alive. Furthermore, young children would be unlikely to understand that living things adapt to their environment: Adaptation is a fairly abstract concept, and it is not readily apparent in children's everyday experiences. Most children probably learn about the importance of adaptation for living things from systematic science instruction at school rather than from their informal experiences outside of school.

Observing Children and Adolescents in Classroom Settings: Observation #9

AUTHOR'S CHAIR

Brief Description: Several students in a second-grade class read the stories they have written about field day events earlier in the week, and their classmates critique their work.

Relevant Chapters: Chapters 12, 13, 14, and the chapter "Learning in the Content Areas" (the last of these chapters is on the Companion Website and in the *Study Guide and Reader*)

Duration: The video segment lasts approximately 9 minutes.

Location: The segment begins approximately $43\frac{1}{2}$ minutes into the video.

Accompanying Materials: Three Observation Records (Handouts MG.12, MG.13, and MG.14) are located in the "Handouts" section near the end of this manual.

Using the Video with Chapter 12

You can use the video to give students an opportunity to examine a teacher's strategies for motivating children and encouraging self-regulation; in doing so, you will draw on material from Chapter 10 as well as Chapter 12.

Before you begin: Explain that these second graders recently participated in their school's end-of-year field day; the following day, they wrote stories about some of the day's events. Today the class is conducting an "Author's Chair," in which various students present their work and their classmates provide feedback.

Distribute Handout MG.12 (Observation Record for "Author's Chair" — Motivation and Self-Regulation) and review the questions that your students should consider as they watch both the children and the teacher.

After the video: Ask your students to share their analyses related to each of the questions on the Observation Record. Some possible responses to the questions are as follows:

What the *Students* Are Doing	
Look for...	Record Your Observations of the Students
Intrinsic Motivation What behaviors and/or statements suggest that the students are intrinsically motivated during this activity?	Several students seem eager to read their stories to the class. The students seem genuinely attentive to their classmates' stories. The authors don't seem to mind having their work critiqued, indicating that their focus may be more on mastery goals than on performance goals.

Extrinsic Motivation What conditions in the classroom may be fostering some extrinsic motivation during this activity?	Because their writing is so "public," most of the students probably have some concern about how they appear to their classmates; thus, they probably have performance goals as well as mastery goals. The students are getting praise from their teacher and classmates. Praise can promote either intrinsic or extrinsic motivation, depending on the extent to which it enhances students' sense of competence, on the one hand, or diminishes their sense of self-determination, on the other. Most of the praise appears to be competence-affirming rather than controlling, and so it probably promotes intrinsic motivation rather than extrinsic motivation.
What the *Teacher* Is Doing	
Look for...	Record Your Observations of the Teacher
Motivational Strategies What strategies is the teacher using to motivate her students?	She fosters internal attributions by implying that becoming a good writer is within students' control. For example, she says, "Our job is to help [Lindsey] become a better writer. Give her, maybe, a compliment and something she can do to be a better writer." She finds good things to say about each student's story, and she is specific about what she praises. For instance, she says, "Something else I liked about Elizabeth's writing: She told what she liked, and she told *why* she liked it. Notice this ..." (she point out a particular sentence in Elizabeth's story). She asks classmates to offer two kinds of feedback: things that they liked about a story (which should enhance the student's sense of competence) and ways that they could make the student become a better writer (which should focus attention on a mastery goal). She models enthusiasm for good writing. She questions students who offer vague feedback so that they provide more specific information about what is good about a story. She keeps Elizabeth on task when Andrew gets up to read his story: "Now, Elizabeth, boys and girls gave you good feedback, now we need your help on helping Andrew." She points out that learning to write is an ongoing process: "... all of your writing could probably stand a little review, and when we finish today, I'd like for you to go back and look at your writing."

Strategies for Promoting Self-Regulation What strategies does the teacher use to help her students become more self-regulating?	By focusing students' attention on helping their classmates become better writers, she fosters internal, controllable attributions. Students who attribute their failures to such controllable factors as lack of effort or ineffective learning strategies are more likely to work hard, persist in the face of failure, and seek help when they need it. By giving specific feedback regarding what she likes about the stories, and by encouraging classmates to give equally specific feedback, she provides criteria by which students will be able to evaluate their own writing in the future. She uses suggestions and rationales more than direct commands. For example, she says, "I thought Eric's comment was very well said—that he felt like, by listening to your story, that he was actually there. And that's exactly what a good writer wants you to feel like."

Using the Video with Chapter 13 or "Learning in the Content Areas"

You can use the video to provide an opportunity for students to examine children's writing skills and to observe how an interactive approach to instruction (in this case, an "author's chair") offers a real audience for, and encourages constructive criticism of, children's writing.

Before you begin: Explain that these second graders recently participated in their school's end-of-year field day; the following day, they wrote stories about some of the events. Today the class is conducting an "Author's Chair," in which students present their work and their classmates provide feedback. Four students—Lindsey, Liz, Elizabeth, and Andrew—read their stories to the class. The teacher also shows Elizabeth's and Andrew's stories on an overhead projector.

Distribute Handout MG.13 (Observation Record for "Author's Chair" — Literacy and Peer Feedback) and review the questions that your students should consider as they watch both the children and the teacher. If you have time, play the video twice, asking your students to consider what the *children* are doing the first time through and what the *teacher* is doing the second time through.

After the video: Ask your students to share their analyses related to each of the questions on the Observation Record. Some possible responses to the questions are as follows:

What the *Students* Are Doing	
Look for...	Record Your Observations of the Students
Writing Skills What strengths and weaknesses do you see in the students' writing skills?	Lindsey's, Liz's, and Andrew's stories convey a sense of emotion and excitement, as well as some attention to detail. For example, Lindsey writes, "I was on the starting line, Grace tightly gripping my ankles." Liz writes, "My heart was pounding," and "My legs were shaking." Andrew writes, "..swet was driping from my head," and "I had a big smile on my face." Elizabeth's story is essentially a list of various things she liked about field day, reflecting a knowledge-telling approach. In contrast, Lindsey tried to create a mood, reflecting some degree of knowledge transforming. (The distinction between knowledge-telling and knowledge-transforming is described in the "Learning in the Content Areas" chapter.) The children are writing in complete sentences and show considerable knowledge of correct spelling, punctuation, and capitalization. However, we see some spelling errors (Elizabeth writes "whip crem" for *whipped cream* and "ballon" for *balloon*, and Andrew writes "swet was driping" for *sweat was dripping*). In addition, Andrew does not always capitalize or use punctuation (quotation marks, commas) when he should.
Types of Peer Feedback What things do students focus on when they critique the authors' stories?	They describe their emotional reactions to the stories. They comment on the realism of the stories. Eric says, "I kinda felt like I was right there." Francie says, "I liked it when you said, 'I was shaking,' because I could just see you shaking. That's the feeling I got when I was ..." (she relates Liz's story to her own experiences at field day). They described the inferences they could draw based on clues in Lindsey's story: They knew it was about a wheelbarrow race because of the words "Grace tightly gripping my ankles." "I think she [Elizabeth] had a really good title." With a show of hands, many students give Elizabeth a rating of 5. The students make some corrections regarding punctuation and capitalization.

What the *Teacher* Is Doing	
Look for...	Record Your Observations of the Teacher
Scaffolding In what ways does the teacher guide the students in their critiques of the authors?	She urges the students to make "criticisms that will help. We call that *constructive* criticism." "You may want to give them a compliment, or you may want to tell them something that will help them become a better writer." "What did [Lindsey] write that told you it was the wheelbarrow race?" "Can you give me an example of an expression that she used, Cedric, that you thought was really well done?" "Give [Elizabeth] some things that she really did well. Not just her handwriting." She asks the students to rate Elizabeth's story on a scale of 1 to 5. She has previously taught the class common editing marks to use during proofreading (e.g., making three lines under letters that need to be uppercase). As Emily edits Andrew's story, she explains the changes being made (explaining quotation marks by saying, "Because that's what Ms. Murphy's saying"; explaining a capitalization by saying, "Because that's the beginning of what she's saying"). When Yuma makes a suggestion, she asks, "Because why?" "Look at this sentence right here, Yuma, and see if you see something."

Types of Teacher Feedback What kinds of feedback does the teacher herself give the students?	"I was really pleased with your stories." "I thought Eric's comment was very well said—that he felt like, by listening to your story, that he was actually there. And that's exactly what a good writer wants you to feel like." "[Liz's story] is very well done, just like the other two you've heard." "I liked that too. I could just see Liz hitting that pie thing in her face. Very well said." "Something else I liked about Elizabeth's writing: She told what she liked, and she told why she liked it." "I liked when you had your conversation with Clayton. I thought that was pretty cool." More generally, the teacher has at least one positive thing to say about each of the four stories. "So, boys and girls, all of your writing could probably stand a little review, and when we finish today, I'd like for you to go back and look at your writing."

Following are additional questions you may want to ask at the end of the videotape:

- In her story, Liz says that field day was "my funnest day of the year." What phenomenon does the word *funnest* reflect? (This question draws on material in the section "Linguistic Development" in Chapter 2.)

  Liz adds the suffix *-est* to create the superlative form of *fun*. *Funnest* is not a word; the correct superlative is *most fun*. Liz is showing *overregularization* when she applies the *-est* rule to a situation where it is not appropriate.

- Do you think that an "author's chair" is an effective approach for improving students' writing skills? Why or why not?

  Students' responses are likely to vary considerably. Following are several ideas that might be addressed during the discussion:
  - The approach gives children a real audience for whom to write and thus makes writing a more authentic activity.
  - Students can model various writing strategies for one another.
  - The approach encourages children to reflect on and revise their writing.

Using the Video with Chapter 14

You can use the video to show strategies for creating an effective classroom climate.

Before you begin: Explain that these second graders recently participated in their school's end-of-year field day; the following day, they wrote stories about some of the day's events. Today the class is conducting an "Author's Chair," in which various students present their work and their classmates provide feedback.

Distribute Handout MG.14 (Observation Record for "Author's Chair" — Classroom Climate) and review the questions that your students should consider as they watch both the children and the teacher.

After the video: Ask your students to share their analyses related to each of the questions on the Observation Record. Some possible responses to the questions are as follows:

What the *Teacher* Is Doing	
Look for...	Record Your Observations of the Teacher
Communicating acceptance, respect, and caring What strategies does the teacher use to show that she genuinely likes and respects her students?	She praises students for the things they have done well in their writing; she also identifies the *specific* things they have done well. She praises students for offering helpful critiques of one another's work (e.g., "I thought Eric's comment was very well said—that he felt like, by listening to your story, that he was actually there. And that's exactly what a good writer wants you to feel like"). She communicates a genuine interest in helping each student improve.
Promoting a sense of community What strategies does the teacher use to promote a sense that students have shared goals and are mutually respectful and supportive of one another's efforts?	Her introduction to the activity communicates an emphasis on helping one another learn: "As we listen, I want us to be a good audience and give our readers some good criticisms, but criticisms that can help. We call that *constructive* criticism.... As you listen to a friend, you may want to give them a compliment, or you may want to tell them something that will help them be a better writer." She continually reiterates the focus on helping one another (e.g., "Let's help [Elizabeth] see some good things about her writing").

What the *Students* Are Doing	
Look for...	Record Your Observations of the Students
Psychological safety What behaviors suggest that students feel psychologically "safe" in the classroom?	Many students are volunteering to read their work to the class. Many students willingly offer both positive and negative feedback. The story authors seem comfortable hearing their peers' constructive criticisms.

Observing Children and Adolescents in Classroom Settings: Observation #10

THE SCARLET LETTER

Brief Description: A high school English class discusses Nathaniel Hawthorne's *The Scarlet Letter*. The discussion focuses on the motives, beliefs, and actions of two characters, Reverend Arthur Dimmesdale and Hester Prynne. The teacher encourages multiple perspectives about what these two characters may be thinking and feeling.

Relevant Chapter: Chapter 3

Duration: The video lasts approximately $5^1/_2$ minutes.

Location: The video clip begins approximately 53 minutes into the video.

Accompanying Materials: An Observation Record (Handout MG.15) is located in the "Handouts" section near the end of this manual.

Using the Video with Chapter 3

You can use the video to demonstrate how discussions of literature can capitalize on adolescents' growing capacity for perspective taking and moral reasoning.

Before you begin: Explain that the video depicts a high school English class studying Nathaniel Hawthorne's *The Scarlet Letter*, a novel set in seventeenth century New England. The lesson focuses on two characters, Reverend Arthur Dimmesdale (a stodgy and pious preacher) and Hester Prynne (a young woman whose husband is absent). The two characters have been carrying on an illicit love affair. When Hester becomes pregnant and bears a child, Dimmesdale remains silent about the fact that he is the father.

The teacher has just read a passage in which Dimmesdale (presumably in an effort to portray himself as a moral leader) makes an impassioned speech beseeching Hester to reveal the father of her child. After reading the passage, she asks half of her students to write down their ideas about what Dimmesdale might be thinking during his speech; she asks the other half to write what Hester might be thinking at the same time. She then asks her students to share their ideas with classmates.

Distribute Handout MG.15 (Observation Record for "*The Scarlet Letter* — Social Cognition and Moral Reasoning") and review the questions that your students should consider as they watch the video.

After the video: Ask your students to share their analyses related to each of the questions on the Observation Record. Some possible responses to the questions are as follows:

What the *Students* Are Doing and Saying	
Look for...	Record Your Observations of the Students
Social Cognition What inferences do students make about the thoughts and feelings of story characters?	The students often speculate about the characters' thoughts and feelings. Following are some examples: • "She does love him." • "She's really upset that he doesn't say anything." • "The reason why she isn't saying anything is because no one would believe her ... maybe she's not that way but that's the way I would be. I wouldn't say a word, but every time I saw him, and every time I had to deal with him, that would be such a good way to get him back, just holding my baby and having that big letter on my chest...." • "Maybe he knows that she won't admit it. He's secure in the fact that he can make a speech because he knows that she won't tell." • "I think that Hester almost pities him.... He doesn't have the courage...." • "It's easier for him to lie." • "He is suffering...."
Moral Development What statements reflect a concern with morality?	Issues of morality and personal responsibility for one's actions frequently arise in the discussion. Following are some examples: • "...and him praying for forgiveness...." • "You should confess, then. My peace is made. You must make yours.... You have your own heart and silence to live with." • "Wouldn't Reverend Dimmesdale be put to death if he came out?" • "I don't think he's such a bad guy...He felt really guilty about it."

What the *Teacher* Is Doing and Saying	
Look for...	Record Your Observations of the Teacher
Instructional Strategies How does the teacher encourage perspective taking and moral reasoning?	She asks each of them to look at the situation from either Hester's or Dimmesdale's perspective and to write down what that character might be thinking. She welcomes diverse perspectives, treating each as legitimate. Following are two examples: • "Notice how different that is from how Nicole sees it. Nicole sees her angry ... and kind of resentful." • "That's a great question, too, Matt, and I'm sure we would all answer it differently."

Observing Children and Adolescents in Classroom Settings: Observation #11

KOHLBERG'S STAGES

Brief Description: Four students participate in a moral reasoning task. They listen to an adult describe a cheating dilemma and then give their opinions about what the boy in the vignette should do and why he shouldn't cheat. The responses are portrayed as being in Kohlberg's preconventional level (for the first two students) or conventional level (for the last two students).

Relevant Chapter: Chapter 3

Duration: The video lasts approximately $2^1/_2$ minutes.

Location: The video clip begins approximately 58 minutes into the video.

Accompanying Materials: An Observation Record (Handout MG.16) is located in the "Handouts" section near the end of this manual.

Using the Video with Chapter 3

This video can serve as the basis for discussion about moral reasoning in children and adolescents.

Before you begin: Explain that students will see four children being interviewed regarding their beliefs about what a boy ("Steve") should do when he has not had time to study and, in particular, whether it is OK for him to cheat. Encourage students to focus on the kinds of reasons that children give.

Distribute Handout MG.16 (Observation Record for "Kohlberg's Stages") and review the questions that your students should consider as they listen to the children.

After the video: Ask your students to share their analyses related to each of the questions on the Observation Record. Some possible responses to the questions follow:

What the *Students* Are Doing	
Look for...	Record Your Observations of the Students
Preconventional Moral Reasoning What responses are consistent with preconventional moral reasoning?	The first two children show preconventional moral reasoning. They focus on the consequences of cheating for the story character: • "Because he'll get kicked out." • "The teacher might find out."
Conventional Moral Reasoning What responses are consistent with conventional moral reasoning?	The last two children show conventional moral reasoning. They think that rules should be followed and that cheating is wrong because it violates society's standards for behavior: • "Because he would be getting somebody else's grade instead of his grade." • "He should have been paying attention earlier in the course ... to know what was going on."

Following is an additional question you may want to ask at the end of the videotape:

• How might students respond if they were thinking at a postconventional level?
   Students might state that the general social order would unravel if people cheated; no one could be trusted to do the right thing. They might also refer to abstract rights and principles, such as *fairness*. For instance, they might say that all the children had the same period of time in which to study, making it unfair for the boy to copy. Or they might say it is not fair for the boy to have to work so hard on the job and at school; instead, it would be fair for his teacher to give him an extra day or two to study.

Observing Children and Adolescents in Classroom Settings: Observation #12

BLAINE

Brief Description: An interview is conducted with Blaine, a tenth grader who has a physical disability and a learning disability. Blaine discusses his career objectives, the cause and effects of his disabilities, and his friendships at school.

Relevant Chapters: Chapters 3 and 5

Duration: The video segment lasts approximately 5 $\frac{1}{2}$ minutes.

Location: The segment begins approximately 61 minutes into the video.

Accompanying Materials: An Observation Record (Handout MG.17) is located in the "Handouts" section near the end of this manual.

Using the Video with Chapter 3 or Chapter 5

You can probably most effectively use this video in conjunction with "David," the video segment that immediately follows it. The two boys are friends, and the separate segments explore their individual perspectives on the friendship.

Before you begin: Explain that a tenth grader is being interviewed about his career goals, his experiences at school, his disability, and his friendships. Ask students to listen and watch for evidence of Blaine's self-perceptions and social skills.

Distribute Handout MG.17 (Observation Record for "Blaine") and review the questions that your students should consider as they listen to student.

After the video: Ask your students to share their analyses related to each of the questions on the Observation Record. Some possible responses to the questions are as follows:

What the *Student* Is Doing and Saying	
Look for...	Record Your Observations of the Student
Self-Perceptions What hypotheses can you form about Blaine's self-concept, self-esteem, and/or self-efficacy?	He wants to become a teacher; apparently he has a sense of self-efficacy that he can achieve this goal. He knows that he has a lot of friends and so sees himself as a likable individual. Although he wishes he could walk, he seems to appreciate the abilities he does have. He says, "I enjoy life, and I'm going to keep on enjoying it."
Social Skills and Prosocial Development What social skills does Blaine appear to have? What evidence of prosocial development do you see?	He smiles readily, appears to maintain eye contact, and carries on a good conversation with the interviewers. He states that he wants to become a teacher so that he can help others, including those without disabilities. For instance, he says, "That's really what I want to do is help other people become better people." He is concerned that some of his peers treat other students with disabilities poorly. He says, "Well, I'd like to change some people getting . . . ah . . . what people may not be saying hi to people that have problems, or ignoring them. It kind of hurts me to see that. I don't like that, really." He himself has not experienced such treatment: "No, I really haven't felt that way. I feel like people have been very nice to me, and I really haven't felt that way." If you have also shown the "David" segment, students might make the following observation as well: David says, "Kids like Blaine always seem to be in better moods. They're happy, and just little things you can do for them, they get more excited than my other friends would." In other words, Blaine appears to reinforce others' kindnesses toward him.

Observing Children and Adolescents in Classroom Settings: Observation #13

DAVID

Brief Description: An interview is conducted with David, a high school senior. David discusses his friendships with students who have disabilities, and especially with Blaine, who is featured in the preceding video segment.

Relevant Chapters: Chapters 3 and 5

Duration: The video segment lasts approximately 10 minutes.

Location: The segment begins approximately 67 minutes into the video.

Accompanying Materials: An Observation Record (Handout MG.18) is located in the "Handouts" section near the end of this manual.

Using the Video with Chapter 3 or 5

You can probably best use this video in conjunction with "Blaine," the segment that immediately precedes it. David and Blaine are friends, and the separate interviews explore their individual perspectives on their friendship. Particular attention in this segment is given to David's reasons for befriending students with disabilities and the benefits he derives from such friendships.

Before you begin: Explain that this high school senior is being interviewed about his career hopes, his experiences at school, and his friendships with Blaine and other students who have disabilities.

Distribute Handout MG.18 (Observation Record for "David") and review the questions that your students should consider as they listen to David. If you have already shown the "Blaine" segment, you might encourage your students to add any additional insights about Blaine on the Observation Record for Blaine.

After the video: Ask your students to share their analyses related to each of the questions on the Observation Record. Some possible responses to the questions are as follows:

What the *Student* Is Doing and Saying	
Look for...	Record Your Observations of the Student
Self-Perceptions What hypotheses can you form about David's self-concept, self-esteem, and/or self-efficacy?	He has considerable self-efficacy about his ability to play basketball; he mentions that he has been on the varsity basketball team for three years. He appears somewhat modest when he says, "Not as good as I should be doing, but I do my best." He describes his school as a challenging one, more specifically as "the private school of the public schools. It's a pretty tough high school, and every year it gets harder and harder." However, David apparently believes that he has been able to rise to the challenge.
Social Skills and Prosocial Development What social skills does David appear to have? What evidence of prosocial development do you see?	He shows well-developed social skills: "It's not something that's organized, it's just something that consciously I try to be a more friendly guy, try to be around. It's not hard, just being friendly to Blaine, that's not tough at all. Just getting along, and making sure things are going all right." He feels confident initiating a conversation with someone he does not know (e.g., a student with a disability). For instance, he says, "It all starts by introducing yourself ... maybe getting on a name-to-name basis...." He shows concern about contributing to the better good of humanity; for instance, he says, "Everyone's given certain things that they work with in their life, and some people have disabilities or hardships in some way. I guess it just makes sense, it's better, I guess, if we can use what we've been given to help other people who have hardships or maybe aren't as strong in other areas. The whole works out better if people put in what they've been given." He enjoys his friendship with Blaine: "I wouldn't do it if I didn't enjoy it. I mean, it's not something I'm obligated to do. It's not like something I'm getting a grade on. Just that alone shows it's something that's worthwhile, it's fun to do. It's not like I'm giving something up, something I kind of want to do. It's not really a feeling I get out of it. It's just something that's worthwhile."

He explains how, by making a concerted effort to reach out to those with disabilities, he models such behavior for others: "It's contagious, because once your friend sees you having a normal conversation with someone that's in a wheelchair or has a learning disability, then they too think, 'Maybe I can get to know that person.' It just takes the initial step, and once that's taken, the rest is real easy. It's not something that you consciously try to do. It just flows."

He shows considerable perspective-taking ability, in that he tries to see the world as a person with a disability might see it. For example:

- He considers how difficult it must be for a student in a wheelchair to get around a large, multistoried school building

- He sees students with disabilities as being very appreciate, as not taking for granted the things that nondisabled students might.

- He perceives students with disabilities to be "normal" teenagers in many respects: "...I see that there's not some huge barrier that separates us. It's just a normal teenager talking to someone who might be in a wheelchair. It's not something that separates us so that we can't have a normal teenage conversation. It's just two friends getting along. Same as any other kid."

Following are additional questions you may want to ask at the end of the videotape:

- Is David unique in his social sensitivity and understanding?

  Students might come to different conclusions about David's qualities, perhaps raising issues such as these:

  - David's apparent self-confidence in social situations has encouraged him to seek out relationships with students who have disabilities, and those relationships may, in turn, have fostered greater perspective taking.

  - Many students are likely to perceive David as being somewhat advanced in his perspective taking and in his commitment to contributing what he can to the greater good of society.

- Think back to the textbook's discussion of moral and prosocial development. What factors promote development in these areas?

  Students might recall factors such as these:

  - Emergence of abstract reasoning ability

  - Encounters with moral dilemmas

  - Emergence of such emotions as shame, guilt, empathy, and sympathy

  - Integration of morality into one's overall sense of identity

  - Induction—that is, hearing reasons why some behaviors are unacceptable

- Exposure to models who exhibit moral behavior (e.g., David might be a good model for his classmates)
- Participation in community service

- <u>What can we learn from Blaine and David?</u>

   Blaine and David have many positive qualities that students may mention. Following are some possible perspectives on this question:

   - Students with disabilities can become an integral part of the social life of a school.
   - Both students have gained something from their relationship. Blaine has benefited from the social support David has given him. David has gained from Blaine's positive attitude and gestures of appreciation.
   - Students such as David can be influential role models for other students.

Observing Children and Adolescents in Classroom Settings: Observation #14

CASTLE DISCUSSION

Brief Description: Two middle school boys describe recent lessons and activities in a unit on medieval Europe. First, an Asian boy in an ESL (English as a Second Language) program is interviewed. He is then joined by a European American boy, who provides further information about the unit and describes social interactions that have been an outgrowth of the unit.

Relevant Chapter: Chapter 4

Duration: The video segment lasts approximately 5 minutes.

Location: The segment begins approximately $75\frac{1}{2}$ minutes into the video.

Accompanying Materials: An Observation Record (Handout MG.19) is located in the "Handouts" section near the end of this manual.

Using the Video with Chapter 4

You can use the video to explore the potential effects of diverse cultural backgrounds on classroom learning, as well as strategies for promoting cross-cultural friendships.

Before you begin: Explain that the video shows two boys being interviewed about what they have learned in a unit on medieval Europe. Shown first is an Asian boy who is learning English as a second language (ESL). Later, a European American boy joins him.

Distribute Handout MG.19 (Observation Record for "Castle Discussion") and review the questions that your students should consider as they watch the children.

After the video: Ask your students to share their analyses related to each of the questions on the Observation Record. Some possible responses to the questions are as follows:

What the *Students* Have Done

Look for...	Record Your Observations of the Students
Effects of Cultural Diversity What difference(s) do you see in what the boys have learned? To what factors might you attribute the difference(s)?	The European American boy speaks with greater confidence about what he has learned than does the Asian boy, although it is impossible to determine from the video alone that one boy has actually learned more than the other. Following are several possible reasons for any differences in what the two boys have learned: • The European American boy has probably had more previous exposure to the nature of life in medieval Europe (knights, castles, etc.). • The European American boy has greater facility with English, the language in which the lesson has been taught. • The boys have sometimes had different activities and assignments; for instance, only the ESL students built the castle. When the Asian boy talks about what he learned during the castle-building activity, he focuses on things that were irrelevant to the main topic of the unit (e.g., he says that he "learned how to build a bridge").
Cross-Cultural Relationships What factors in this situation appear to have promoted cross-cultural relationships?	Although the native English speakers have sometimes been engaged in different activities than the ESL students, both groups have been studying the same topic, and apparently the entire class has made use of what the two groups have accomplished to better understand the subject matter. After the lessons, the boys went to lunch together and played sports. The European American boy tells us, "After we would work on Scotland, we'd always go out and eat lunch together, and we were meeting a lot of new friends. So it worked well. We'd play basketball and football, and everything outside, after lunch." Both boys smile at this point, showing that they apparently enjoyed the opportunities for recreation and companionship. The Asian boy's English proficiency is undoubtedly a factor affecting his relationships with his classmates. As he becomes increasingly able to communicate in English, his relationships should improve in number and quality.

Following is an additional question you may want to ask at the end of the videotape:

- <u>What was your overall impression of the cultural sensitivity of the lesson?</u>
  Students' opinions are likely to vary. Following are examples of issues that may arise:
  - European history may be inherently more interesting to students of European ancestry than to students from other backgrounds.
  - The unit could have been made more multicultural by contrasting medieval Europe with ways of life in other parts of the world (e.g., in Asia, in North America) during the same time period.
  - The native English speakers and ESL students seem to have been working separately for a considerable part of the unit. Greater participation in the *same* activities would probably have yielded both academic and social benefits.

Handouts

The handouts on the following pages are also available on the Instructor's CD *PowerPoint Slides and Supplementary Lectures and Activities*.

Essential Teaching Skills

Evaluate the lesson on the basis of the following criteria:

- **Attitudes**
  - Warmth and Empathy
  - High Expectations
  - Enthusiasm and Energy
  - Modeling

- **Organization**

- **Communication**
  - Precise Terminology
  - Connected Discourse
  - Transition Signals
  - Emphasis

- **Focus**
  - Introductory Focus
  - Sensory Focus
  - Academic Focus

- **Feedback**

- **Monitoring**

- **Questioning**
  - Frequency
  - Equitable Distribution
  - Prompting
  - Wait Time
  - Question Level

- **Review and Closure**

Jeanne Ellis Ormrod
Educational Psychology: Developing Learners 4/E

Observation Record for
"Portfolio" — Motivation and Self-Regulation

What the *Student* Is Doing	
Look for ...	Record Your Observations of the Student
Intrinsic Motivation What does the student do and say to indicate that she is intrinsically motivated to read and write?	
Self-Regulation What behaviors and/or statements indicate that the student is acquiring some self-regulatory strategies related to her reading and writing?	
What the *Teacher* Is Doing	
Look for ...	Record Your Observations of the Teacher
Motivational Strategies What strategies is the teacher using to motivate the student?	

Jeanne Ellis Ormrod
Educational Psychology: Developing Learners 4/E

Observation Record for
"Portfolio" — Self-Assessment

What the *Student* Is Doing	
Look for ...	Record Your Observations of the Student
Self-Assessment What improvements does the student identify in her writing and reading?	

What the *Teacher* Is Doing	
Look for ...	Record Your Observations of the Teacher
Teaching Strategies In what ways does the teacher scaffold the student's efforts to evaluate her own progress?	

Jeanne Ellis Ormrod
Educational Psychology: Developing Learners 4/E

Observation Record for
"Portfolio" — Literacy Development

What the *Student* Is Doing	
Look for ...	Record Your Observations of the Student
Writing Development What developmental changes do you see in the student's writing?	
Reading Development What developmental changes do you see in the student's reading?	

Observation Record for
"Painting Class"

What Questions the *Interviewer* Is Asking	
Look for ...	Record Examples of Questions the Interviewer Asks
Kinds of Questions What kinds of questions does the interviewer ask?	

What Information the *Student* Is Providing	
Look for ...	Record Examples of the Student's Responses to Questions
Student's Responses What kinds of information is the student providing? What kinds of information is she *not* providing?	

Jeanne Ellis Ormrod
Educational Psychology: Developing Learners 4/E

Observation Record for
"Piaget Tasks"

What the *Students* Are Doing	
Look for ...	Record Your Observations of the Students
Preoperational Thought What statements reflect preoperational thinking?	
Concrete Operational Thought What statements reflect concrete operational thinking?	
What the *Teacher* Is Doing	
Look for ...	Record Your Observations of the Teacher
Conservation Tasks What specific tasks does the teacher present to assess students' understanding of conservation?	
Use of Clinical Method What kinds of questions does the teacher ask? Does she ask enough questions to get a full understanding of the students' reasoning?	

Jeanne Ellis Ormrod
Educational Psychology: Developing Learners 4/E

Observation Record for
"Designing Experiments"

What the *Students* Are Doing	
Look for ...	Record Your Observations of the Students
Concrete Operations What behaviors and statements reflect concrete operational thinking?	
Formal Operations What behaviors and statements reflect formal operational thinking?	
What the *Teacher* Is Doing	
Look for ...	Record Your Observations of the Teacher
Scaffolding In what ways does the teacher scaffold the students' reasoning?	
Types of Feedback What kinds of feedback does the teacher give the students about their performance?	

Observation Record for
"Pendulum Presentation"

What the *Students* Are Doing	
Look for ...	Record Your Observations of the Students
Concrete Operations What statements reflect concrete operational thinking?	
Formal Operations What statements reflect formal operational thinking?	
What the *Teacher* Is Doing	
Look for ...	Record Your Observations of the Teacher
Scaffolding In what ways does the teacher scaffold the students' reasoning?	
Types of Feedback What kinds of feedback does the teacher give the students about their performance?	

Jeanne Ellis Ormrod
Educational Psychology: Developing Learners 4/E

Observation Record for
"Birdwatching"

What the *Children* Are Doing	
Look for ...	Record Your Observations of the Children
Interactions with the physical environment In what ways do the children interact with their physical environment?	
Construction of Meaning What understandings do the children construct during the activity?	
What the *Adult* Is Doing	
Look for ...	Record Your Observations of the Adult
Scaffolding In what ways does the teacher scaffold the children's learning?	
Cultural interpretation At what points does the adult pass along her culture's interpretations of what the children are observing?	

Jeanne Ellis Ormrod
Educational Psychology: Developing Learners 4/E

Observation Record for
"Balance Scales"

What the *Students* Are Doing	
Look for ...	Record Your Observations of the Students
Siegler's Strategy 1 What responses consider only the number of weights on each side of the scale?	
Siegler's Strategy 2 What responses consider distance as well as weight but without a precise understanding of how the two factors interrelate?	
Siegler's Strategy 3 What responses reflect a multiplicative relationship between number of weights and distance from the fulcrum?	

Observation Record for
"Yeast Discussion"

What the *Students* Are Doing	
Look for ...	Record Your Observations of the Students
Children's Theories What do the students' comments tell us about their *personal theories* about the nature of life?	
Cognitive Processes What behaviors indicate that the students are probably using effective cognitive processes?	
What the *Teacher* Is Doing	
Look for ...	Record Your Observations of the Teacher
Instructional Strategies What strategies does the teacher use to help the students understand the nature of yeast?	
Cognitive Apprenticeship What strategies does the teacher use to help the students think in ways that scientists think?	

Jeanne Ellis Ormrod
Educational Psychology: Developing Learners 4/E

Observation Record for
"Author's Chair" — Motivation and Self-Regulation

What the *Students* Are Doing	
Look for ...	Record Your Observations of the Students
Intrinsic Motivation What behaviors and/or statements suggest that the students are intrinsically motivated during this activity?	
Extrinsic Motivation What conditions in the classroom may be fostering some extrinsic motivation during this acitivity?	
What the *Teacher* Is Doing	
Look for ...	Record Your Observations of the Teacher
Motivational Strategies What strategies is the teacher using to motivate her students?	
Strategies for Promoting Self-Regulation What strategies does the teacher use to help her students become more self-regulating?	

Jeanne Ellis Ormrod
Educational Psychology: Developing Learners 4/E

Observation Record for
"Author's Chair" — Literacy and Peer Feedback

What the *Students* Are Doing	
Look for ...	Record Your Observations of the Students
Writing Skills What strengths and weaknesses do you see in the students' writing skills?	
Types of Peer Feedback What things do students focus on when they critique the authors' stories?	
What the *Teacher* Is Doing	
Look for ...	Record Your Observations of the Teacher
Scaffolding In what ways does the teacher guide the students in their critiques of the authors?	
Types of Teacher Feedback What kinds of feedback does the teacher herself give the students?	

Jeanne Ellis Ormrod
Educational Psychology: Developing Learners 4/E

Observation Record for
"Author's Chair" — Classroom Climate

What the *Teacher* Is Doing	
Look for ...	Record Your Observations of the Teacher
Communication, acceptance, respect, and caring What strategies does the teacher use to show that she genuinely likes and respects her students?	
Promoting a sense of community What strategies does the teacher use to promote a sense that students have shared goals and are mutually respectful and supportive of one another's efforts?	
What the *Students* Are Doing	
Look for ...	Record Your Observations of the Students
Psychological safety What behaviors suggest that students feel psychologically "safe" in the classroom?	

Jeanne Ellis Ormrod
Educational Psychology: Developing Learners 4/E

Observation Record for
"The Scarlet Letter" — Social Cognition and Moral Reasoning

What the *Students* Are Doing and Saying	
Look for ...	Record Your Observations of the Students
Social Cognition What inferences do students make about the thoughts and feelings of story characters?	
Moral Development What statements reflect a concern with morality?	

What the *Teacher* Is Doing and Saying	
Look for ...	Record Your Observations of the Teacher
Instructional Strategies How does the teacher encourage perspective taking and moral reasoning?	

Jeanne Ellis Ormrod
Educational Psychology: Developing Learners 4/E

Observation Record for
"Kohlberg's Stages"

What the *Students* Are Doing	
Look for ...	Record Your Observations of the Students
Preconventional Moral Reasoning What responses are consistent with preconventional moral reasoning?	
Conventional Moral Reasoning What responses are consistent with conventional moral reasoning?	

Jeanne Ellis Ormrod
Educational Psychology: Developing Learners 4/E

Observation Record for
"Blaine"

What the *Student* Is Doing and Saying	
Look for ...	Record Your Observations of the Student
Self-Perceptions What hypotheses can you form about Blaine's self-concept, self-esteem, and/or self-efficacy?	
Social Skills and Prosocial Development What social skills does Blaine appear to have? What evidence of prosocial development do you see?	

Jeanne Ellis Ormrod
Educational Psychology: Developing Learners 4/E

Observation Record for
"David"

What the *Student* Is Doing and Saying	
Look for ...	Record Your Observations of the Student
Self-Perceptions What hypotheses can you form about David's self-concept, self-esteem, and/or self-efficacy?	
Social Skills and Prosocial Development What social skills does David appear to have? What evidence of prosocial development do you see?	

Observation Record for
"Castle Discussion"

What the *Students* Have Done	
Look for ...	Record Your Observations of the Students
Effects of Cultural Diversity What difference(s) do you see in what the boys have learned? To what factors might you attribute the difference(s)?	
Cross-Cultural Relationships What factors in this situation appear to have promoted cross-cultural relationships?	

Jeanne Ellis Ormrod
Educational Psychology: Developing Learners 4/E

Transparency Masters

The transparency masters on the following pages are also available on the Instructor's CD
PowerPoint Slides and Supplementary Lectures and Activities.

The Companion Website for the textbook can be found at:

www.prenhall.com/ormrod

Features of the Companion Website:

- Navigation bar

- Course syllabus

- Chapter features:
    - Central questions
    - Chapter glossary
    - Internet sites related to chapter content
    - Self-test items (with hints and feedback)

- Supplementary Readings

- Link to Student Artifact Library

- Message board

- Feedback button

Jeanne Ellis Ormrod
Educational Psychology: Developing Learners 4/E

Simulations in Educational Psychology and Research CD

- The Pendulum Experiment

- Assessing Moral Reasoning

- Bartlett's Ghosts

- Intuitive Physics

- Assessment in the Balance

Each simulation is designed to be self-explanatory. General directions are as follows:

1. Insert the CD into your computer and click on the diamond-shaped "Sims" icon.

2. Read each frame, make any response called for, and then click on either the arrow or "Next" button that appears in the lower right corner.

3. Video clips are built into each of the simulations. When you see what appears to be a photograph with several buttons immediately below it, click on the right-pointing arrow just below the "photo" to begin the video.

4. If you get to a frame called "Opportunities for Learning," click on the "Educational Psychology" button to learn about educational implications related to the simulation.

$$26$$
$$-\ \underline{17}$$

- "You take the 6 and the 7 off . . . and then take off 10, and that would be 10, and take off 7 more, and that would be 3, and add the 6 back on and then that would be 9."

- "I took 10 off the 20 and that was 10, and I took 6 off the 7 and that was 0, and then I took 1 off the 10 and that was 9."

- "10 take off from 20 is 10, and then add a 6 on, it's 16, minus 7, it's 9."

Jeanne Ellis Ormrod
Educational Psychology: Developing Learners 4/E

$$9$$
$$\underline{+\ 6}$$

- "If 9 were a 10 and the 6 were a 5 . . . (Teacher: Okay, and what would your answer be?) . . . 15."

- "I took 1 away from the 6 and added it to the 9, that would make the 9 be 10, and 5 and 10 is 15."

- "I knew 9 plus 7 was 16, so I took away 1, that made 15."

- "I took 3 off the 9, made that 6, and that would be 12, and then add 3 on, and that would be 15."

Jeanne Ellis Ormrod
Educational Psychology: Developing Learners 4/E

$$26$$
$$\underline{+\ 5}$$

- "I took the 1 off the 6 and that was 5, and then I knew 5 and 5 was 30 . . . I mean, five and 5 was 10, and then I knew that was 30, then just added 1."

- "I put the 26 . . . with the 20, and added the 6 and 5 together and that was 11, so I put the 11 onto the 20 and I knew it was 31."

- "I took the 1 off the 26 . . . and then I took 25 and 5 together and it made 30. That extra 1, I put it on, and it made 31."

- "I knew that 26 plus 4 was 30, and add one more to the 4, and then it's 31."s

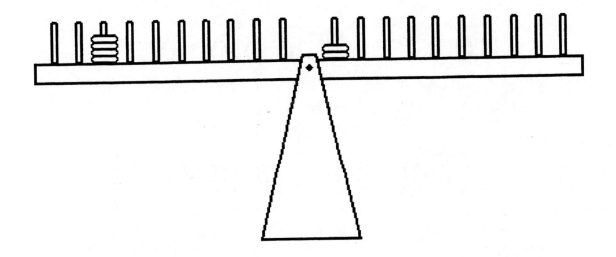

Jeanne Ellis Ormrod
Educational Psychology: Developing Learners 4/E

<u>Steps in Problem Solving</u>

Identify the problem

• • •

Represent the problem

• • •

Select a strategy

• • •

Carry out the strategy

• • •

Evaluate results

Jeanne Ellis Ormrod
Educational Psychology: Developing Learners 4/E

A. Balance Scale

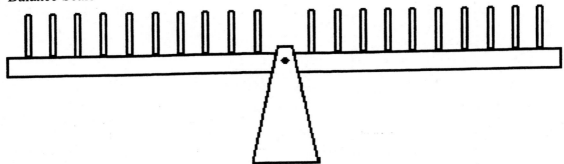

B. Example of how distance compensates for weight

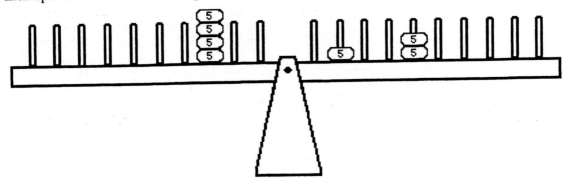

C. Dr. Eggen's initial problem

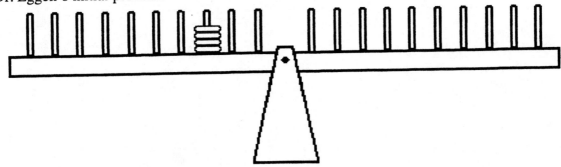

D. Suzanne's solution (with one weight removed from Peg 3)

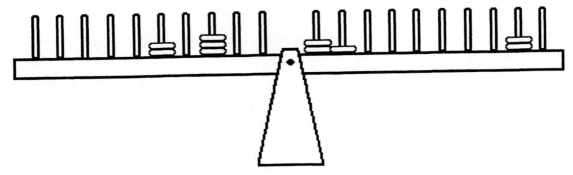

Jeanne Ellis Ormrod
Educational Psychology: Developing Learners 4/E